BÔ YIN RÂ

(JOSEPH ANTON SCHNEIDERFRANKEN)

VOLUME 31

OF THE 32-VOLUME CYCLE

THE GATED GARDEN

LETTERS TO ONE AND TO MANY

For more information about the books of Bô Yin Râ and titles available in English translation visit The Kober Press web site at www.kober.com

THE KOBER PRESS PUBLISHES THE ONLY ENGLISH TRANSLATIONS OF THE BOOKS OF BÔ YIN RÂ AUTHORIZED BY THE KOBER VERLAG, SWITZERLAND. THE KOBER VERLAG PUBLISHES THE BOOKS OF BÔ YIN RÂ IN THE ORIGINAL GERMAN AND HAS PROTECTED THEIR INTEGRITY SINCE THE AUTHOR'S LIFETIME.

BÔ YIN RÂ
(JOSEPH ANTON SCHNEIDERFRANKEN)

LETTERS TO ONE AND TO MANY

TRANSLATED FROM THE GERMAN BY
JAN SCHYMURA, MALKA WEITMAN
AND ERIC STRAUSS

BERKELEY, CALIFORNIA

Eric W. Strauss, Publisher

This book is a translation from the German *Briefe an Einen und Viele* by Bô Yin Râ (J.A. Schneiderfranken), published in 1935 by Kober'sche Verlagsbuchhandlung, Basel-Leipzig

Printed in the United States of America

International Standard Book Number:
978-0-915034-33-8

Typography and composition by BookMatters

Book cover after a design by Bô Yin Râ

CONTENTS

Translators' Note vii
Preface ix
1 What the Soul Possesses 1
2 Needless Fears 7
3 Necessary Confidence 13
4 My Way of Writing 21
5 On Revealing Who I Am 27
6 What One Must Leave Behind 35
7 The Temple of Eternity 41
8 About My Spiritual Nature 49
9 How Spiritual Help Reaches Us 57
10 God Is Not Involved in World Affairs 71
11 How God Grants Help to Individuals 79
12 The Forces of the Soul 87
13 On New Editions of My Books 97

14 Polytheism and the Veneration of Saints 105
15 The Nature of Life in the Light 115
16 True Awakening Is Always Gentle 123
17 Jacob Böhme and the German Mystics . . 131
18 What God Is 139
19 Being and Beingness 149
20 Questions I Do Not Want to Be Asked . . 157
21 The Number Twelve and the Bell Tower Clock 165
22 The Blinders that Must Fall from One's Eyes 175
23 No Two Individuals Are the Same Before God 183
24 On Professing Before Others 193
25 Masters Who Have Fallen 203
26 Radiant Stones and Substances 211
27 The Need to Devalue Suffering 219
28 The Nature of Blessing and How It Is Bestowed 231
29 The Timeless Nature of Eternity 241
30 Surrender and Inner Stillness 249
Conclusion 257

TRANSLATORS' NOTE

What Cannot Be Translated from the German Original

*"...if one would derive the fullest benefit from studying the books I wrote to show the way into the Spirit, one has to read them in the original; even if this should require learning German."**

No translation can ever do full justice to the particular qualities inherent in another language, but Bô Yin Râ had an additional reason for urging his readers to read his works in the original German, if at all possible. He tells us that he has chosen his words, not according to personal taste, but "...in accordance with certain spiritual laws that govern the power inherent in sounds." Bô Yin Râ often refers to this "sound-magic" that he embedded into the original German—the special rhythms and spiritual power of sounds that has guided his choice of words.

Although the English translations published by The Kober Press strive to recreate the beauty and feeling of the original German publications, our translations can only hint at, but cannot recreate, the sound-magic Bô Yin Râ embedded in them.

---

*Translated from the article "Jedem Antwort" (Answers to Everyone), originally written in 1933 and republished in *Nachlese,* (1990), Bern: Kober'sche Verlagsbuchhandlung.

PREFACE

IN MY BOOK *Signs Along the Way*, I HAVE made clear the reasons I am against the practice of publishing letters after the author's death. Letters are usually written in response to specific situations and thus can only be correctly understood in context.

I have, of course, no power at all to prevent the publication of my own letters after my death—letters that I wrote to address a specific situation at a specific moment in time and which can only be understood within that context. Since I have no control over what happens to those letters after my death, it would be foolish if, during my lifetime, I were to fret over the possible future misuse of that which belongs to me.

That said, I feel compelled to demonstrate how one can distinguish between those of my letters that are valid only for a specific situation and time and those letters that can be helpful to readers at *any* time because they deal with my teachings, which are timeless in nature.

In the past I wrote many letters of the latter type to many different people, with modifications as appropriate, so certain readers will recognize in this book excerpts from letters that were written to them. I hope, however, that none of them will feel that the sanctity of these letters has been diminished when I make public what was once offered to them alone since, after all, I am offering to a wider public teachings that derive from me. Further, they should bear in mind that, even though the teachings in these letters are timeless and therefore have universal value, they can only serve those individuals who have prepared themselves inwardly and whose souls are able to make use of them.

Answers that I had previously written to many different people in response to their questions are summarized here. After all, there are in this life for those souls still bound to our earth only a certain range of experiences and these lead always to the same questions.

Every single letter in this collection faithfully relates to specific inquiries, comments, or reports sent to me at one time or another. Thus, the matters that moved me to write the letters presented in this book were not invented by me as a pretext to expound on subjects important to me.

These sample letters are based on private letters I once wrote by way of providing needed explanations and counseling to individuals, with the content edited so as to make it suitable for the general readership. Thus, one could say that the content of this book had already been written long ago, but only needed to be shaped into this final form.

Long gone are the days when, in addition to fulfilling the rigorous spiritual obligations made known to me by the realm of timeless Spirit, I could work productively almost without pause from sunrise to sunset. Then, after quickly eating a light meal, I was able to sit at my desk until the dawn of a new day, answering letters. After a short, deep sleep I could be found standing in front of my easel or shaping my manuscripts into the final form that would allow them to be most accessible to those waiting for the Light. Today I do not look back and ask whether the degree of my dedication to answering letters was imprudent; what is true is that my physical body finally reacted so badly to the taxing treatment it had received over many years that I was forced to forego this activity.

I wrote the letters in this book by hand despite the physical hindrances that interfere with my writing these days—just the way I used to write their prototypes before I was beset by these plaguing obstructions. There is nothing exceptional here as everything I have published to date has first been handwritten in ink. The manuscript I submit to the typesetter has always been based on a handwritten first manuscript which, unfortunately, cannot conceal the physical strain handwriting now causes me and falls far short of my own standards for my handwriting. So that my handwriting can be understood, I have no choice but to dictate for later transcription those rare and unavoidable letters which I occasionally still try to write.

These days my handwriting must, as far as it is still possible, be reserved solely for my texts of spiritual teaching for which a handwritten manuscript is unavoidable. This book is an example of such a teaching text: In it my teaching is given in the form of correspondence. All readers who feel that these letters truly speak to them may regard each one as having been addressed to them personally, even if there has never been any private correspondence between us.

May the sample letters I present here serve as guides for those who have made themselves ready for the teachings and may they alone feel themselves addressed by my words.

Back!—back with all of you
who deliberately
and eagerly
crowd around everything
not meant for your greedy
unclean animal souls
bound up in your mortal bodies.

I have not come
for you to mistake me
as one of your kind—
you, the ones I do *not* call.

What I bring
is only offered to those
who are conscious of
their pure eternal soul—

to those who are disciplined and sober
who reflect before speaking
those who cleanse their hands
before touching
what you only sully.

❧

Tell us: Who are you?
We need to know you!
What is the right name
to give to your kind?

I am a radiant beam
and its everlasting light.
I am a word
that speaks itself.
I am a sword
and a protective shield.
I am a creator
and the creation.
I am a ring
and the stone in its setting.
I am the vintner
and I am the wine.
I am the tree trunk
and also its branch.
I am a human
who knows how to strike
luminous sparks from timeless ice.

What I have come to bring
one offers first to those
who speak one's tongue
before passing it on
also to those who speak foreign tongues
to take in as much as they can.

If you my compatriots
do not want what I offered first to you
you will later—
believe me, I know—
secure for yourselves from a distance
what could have been yours today...
like Night's companions
timidly, on tiptoes.

LETTER ONE

WHAT THE SOUL POSSESSES

YOU TELL ME THAT MUCH OF WHAT YOU read in *The Book on the Living God* feels to you to already have been your soul's possession for a long time, even though you have not yet been able to find the words to express what your soul can sense. Although you did not speak in detail about the passages in the book that gave you the sense of reading about something already familiar, I assume that in the various chapters that you had never read before, you came upon words that expressed what you had already experienced within yourself.

If I understand you correctly, you have truly recognized in my writings something that is already yours: this because your soul issues from the same primordial Ground of Being as mine. I seek nothing other in my books than to portray this eternal Reality, which is unaffected by all mortal opinions and beliefs and which is the birthright and primal possession of every soul. In life on earth, however, dominated as it is by the senses and demands of the physical plane, the memory of eternal Reality is usually forced into the background of consciousness until all that remains is a distant, faded, dreamlike recollection.

Viewed with all this in mind, your assertion is not at all surprising. It simply tells me that certain of my words were able to stimulate the suppressed memory of your soul to the point where you recognized that I was expressing in words an experience that was already your own inner possession. When you say that reading my words brings you joy because they enable you to relive, whenever you wish, certain familiar states of your soul, this confirms my explanation. As to that "strange yet comforting feeling" that comes from realizing that you have attained certainty about an inner region that had previously seemed to be closed to you, do not be at all concerned. You give yourself good counsel when you acknowledge that you still very much *need* my words and that, for the time being, you find them to be the only useful keys to the treasures stored in your soul.

I look forward to hearing more from you as to how you are able to use these keys to serve you. However, you should not expect to enter into a regular exchange of letters with me. I would have to replicate myself several times over in order to satisfy even just a few of those who hope that I will reply to their letters. It is not the limitations of my "precious time," mentioned ad nauseam in many of the letters I receive, which prevents me from writing down all the answers I would sincerely love to give but, rather, the limitations of my physical energy, which has long been overstrained beyond all acceptable measure. That said, if I find that you have misunderstood something significant in one of your reports about your progress—which, after all, I have asked you for—I shall do what I can to provide you with clarification.

May heaven bless you!

LETTER TWO

NEEDLESS FEARS

OUR ABILITY TO FEEL THINGS WITH THE soul can be hindered by a kind of inhibited receptivity that is analogous, on the physical level, to what one might call signs of fatigue. What you describe in your present letter is clearly a description of this kind of fatigue.

You told me how joyful it was for you to read my descriptions of the experiences you have had within your soul. The excitement you felt at hearing those experiences put into words so accurately and for the first time evidently caused you to ignore many of the other points I made in my book. You simply did not concern yourself with what was unfamiliar to you.

As you yourself said, this initial excitement was "exceptionally strong and long-lasting." However, no human being is able to continuously sustain such inner elation with the same intensity. To keep from over-taxing our physical organism, even the strongest inner excitement must of necessity subside. You, however, refused to accept this truth, believing that a repeated reading of the sentences which had such a stimulating effect on you would lead to ever renewed joy.

It did not occur to you that you would simply overtire yourself. Once you became fatigued, those of my words that deal with matters *unfamiliar* to you suddenly rose up before you. In your letter, you described this occurrence as "strange" and "disturbing" but, although it may have felt this way to you, this need not be the only way to think of it. You merely became aware of the unfamiliar things you had missed during your first reading. At that time you immersed yourself in familiar things while glossing over the rest.

Each time you reread one of my books you will have a similar experience, even if you believe you have already almost memorized the book. You will be astonished that, although you thought you knew everything there is to know about its contents, you will always encounter something new.

These books describe all the states of consciousness possible for the soul. Every time readers pick up a book again, they find new meaning in its pages. This is because the state of consciousness of *their* soul has changed and thus their perception of what is written is different. There is no reason, therefore, for you to doubt that it is possible to continuously expand and deepen the ability to experience with your soul. But you must be patient, just as patience is needed if one wishes to play a musical instrument or master a foreign language.

You may have assumed you had more understanding of what we human beings are able to experience in our souls than you actually had and must now come to realize that there is incomparably more to experience than you had thought possible. If your present doubts about your ability to expand your soul keep you, in the future, from the tendency to overestimate what you already are able to achieve inwardly—take heart. Your current disappointment is the surest sign that you shall one day—even if it should take longer than you might wish—find yourself awake in the realm of soul. Be patient, therefore, and realize that in order to reach your goal much dedication is required.

Because you have removed yourself
too far from the center of your own being
and dreaming
were enthralled by the images in your dreams
the bond that bonded you with God
loosened and fell away.
And now, bound only to illusion and folly
you have drifted away from who you are.

Trapped inside your dreaming self
you have called out to God.
Stifled by this self
you lie before the very steps
that could, within your self,
raise you upward towards God
out of darkness and uncertainty
to your new life.

LETTER THREE

NECESSARY CONFIDENCE

YOU MAY DOUBT EVERYTHING—EVEN me—but never doubt your ability to awaken in the light of the soul. Every sentence in your last letter expressed this sort of doubt and it is doubt that can, indeed, hinder your awakening.

You write that in my last letter I suggested that you had overestimated how far you have come on the path—and you have trouble reconciling that assessment with what I said you are capable of attaining. However, the *potential* for future development that I see in you is innate in every person. It has nothing to do with what you have or have not already achieved, and does not depend on what I or anyone else thinks of you.

When you have progressed as far as you must to have attained the goal I described to you, it will become clear to you that I have not overestimated your abilities—even though it seems that way to you today. Your present attempt to minimize the progress you have made is merely a reaction to your previous overestimation of how far you had developed inwardly. The pendulum has now swung in the opposite direction.

You must calm yourself and find your inner center.

Like all seekers at the beginning of their journey, you take your evaluation of your abilities, and others' opinions of you, too seriously. Perhaps this observation on my part will allay your fear that, when I give you hope that you can indeed reach the goal you seek, I am expecting too much of you. All this worry is somewhat like a childhood disease that would only be a cause for concern if it did not dissipate of its own accord with the passage of time.

Today you find yourself at the beginning of a path whose goal you may be able to see in your mind's eye, but whose reality you can only guess at. Your path is *within* you and only within yourself will you arrive at your soul's destination. But beware, within you also are the forest ponds, swamps, and puddles in which you have so enjoyed contemplating your own reflection.

You surely know what I mean, even if I deliberately do not use psychological terms to describe this way of viewing yourself. You must wean yourself completely of such self-centered contemplation and your attachment to a certain self-image, if you are to stay steadfast on your inner journey and not lose sight of the goal.

Your perception of yourself is not who you truly are: Your *true* self always remains the same, regardless of whether you like the reflection you see of yourself or not. Know, however, that whenever you accept that a particular reflection of yourself—as seen from the perspective of your current state of consciousness—is truly who you are, you will root yourself to that spot. You will remain stuck in a place from which you should be moving on.

The importance you attach to yourself and others here on earth, to your position in society and its significance, to whether it is yours to command others or to obey commands, and a thousand other matters considered important in this life to which you feel fettered and may not even wish to be freed from—these are all matters between birth and death. But that which is eternal in your own soul is waiting to be sought and found by you and is unaffected by everything you consider so important here on earth.

By all means strive for everything you value highly in your earthly existence but, while doing so, do not forget that which is eternal in you.

Your physical body is the workshop in which you may shape and perfect your eternal self. It offers you the tools you need for this work but it is *you* who must use it to create the form of your timeless self.

Unless you have created this spiritual form out of that which is eternal in you, it will not be possible for the consciousness of your spiritual being and the consciousness of your mortal being to merge into one greater consciousness. If you were limited to seeing only from the perspective of the physical human being, fettered as it is to our earthly, animal senses, your eternal nature would forever remain foreign to you. This is because your physical being is completely unaware of anything eternal in itself and, at most, can only be persuaded to "believe" in its existence—rather than to experience it directly. Once you have created the spiritual form suitable for it, however, you will attain permanent consciousness of your eternal nature. Only *you* can create this form and for this you must maintain the appropriate intention and inner bearing.

LETTER FOUR

MY WAY OF WRITING

YOUR STRONG COMMITMENT AND RE-solve to progress on the path was so clear in your last letter that it would not feel right to me to leave you without an answer any longer than necessary. I shall therefore temporarily put on hold many of my tasks so that you may hear from me immediately.

I understand your concern that your "dry and, as a result of professional demands, predominantly rational" nature might impede your ability to make the progress you so earnestly desire. I shall do my best to express myself in ways that may bridge the distance between my writing style and the style you might require for understanding. Please feel free to describe any difficulties you may have in understanding me.

It would be helpful for me to learn how I can revise things I have written so that they will be easier for you to fully comprehend. I am as willing as the next person to learn from a serious and rational person like yourself where I may have left questions unanswered or have asked my readers to attempt tasks that are beyond their capacity to master.

You have mentioned the "unusual style of writing" in my books and here I must tell you, as a sober fact, that I have never yet written anything where I was free to *choose* the words and form of my expression. Whatever you see in writing always had to be expressed only in the way that you see it in print. I have never tried to find my own personal style of expression. Rather, I have always chosen my words in accordance with certain spiritual laws that govern the power inherent in sounds.

Had I a trace of literary ambition it would have been easy for me to have made use of a more contemporary writing style. But not only am I far from any literary striving: my whole love and attention is with every word that I use—with every letter of the alphabet that I write down—so much so that I have no time to think about how what I am obliged to say could be expressed in the writing style of my time on this earth. Wherever I find the words I need in contemporary writing style, I use those words; however, when the available words are inadequate, I create the expressions necessary.

Moreover, I cannot write anything that does not feel to me like the spoken word. This explains why the arrangement of sentences and punctuation in my writing may at first glance seem a bit eccentric. Since you are now in possession of what I have written over the course of two decades you will also notice a generous use of dashes of different lengths* in some of the first books published. I used these dashes as a way to indicate shorter or longer pauses between passages, so that they could be perceived as if being spoken. However, because a large number of readers misunderstood my intention, I later kept the use of such signs to a bare minimum.

Despite this, readers should still imagine that the written words are being spoken aloud.

* These dashes have been omitted in the English translations.

Otherwise, they will miss the vital essence that the sentences have to offer to their innermost.

With this, I hope I have responded to all the questions to which I believe I owe you answers. This because you have told me of your resolve to devote a quiet hour every day to allowing the meaning of my books to penetrate more and more deeply—even if your efforts will be guided by your intellect at first.

With regard to the order in which you should study my books, I leave you with complete freedom. However, I do prefer that you read certain books first before moving on to others that require a reasonable understanding of various concepts. That said, whenever you have finished reading one book and are considering which one to read next, I advise you to only choose a book if it strongly appeals from the moment you open it. If you have trouble making headway, it would be better to save that book for later and pick another that seems more appealing in the immediate.

My blessings are with you!

LETTER FIVE

ON REVEALING WHO I AM

THE FACT THAT YOU ONLY MANAGED TO write back to me now, after four months, requires no apology. I know how demanding your professional life is. Aside from that, I assume that you would only ask me questions if they arose after careful examination of my texts—and such examination takes time. When one is forced to continuously exceed one's available energy reserves and when it seems there are scarcely enough hours in each day to meet one's many pressing obligations—as is the case with me—then a period of four months can feel like little more than four days.

I understand that you first had to get an overview of all the books and their individual chapters before you could focus on the particular texts most relevant to your questions.

I am amazed, however, that you were able to gain such an overview in the relatively short space of four months, despite the many other matters that required your attention. Your observations about what you have read confirm to me that you have indeed succeeded in gaining the sought-after overview.

It was a good idea to read my writings in the order in which they were published and I was very pleased to hear that much of what was unclear to you while reading *The Book on the Living God* became clear through reading my later books—as you expected would be the case. I was also impressed by your comments, which showed a sensitivity and refinement of perception. I take note that you were able to read between the lines in the first book I wrote and in several of the following books and saw the struggle it has been for me to reveal myself to the world in my writings. You saw how at first I wrote only reluctantly and in very general terms which concealed more than they revealed. Even today, when it is possible and bearable for me to reveal more, I continue this practice of concealment—and that which I conceal remains hidden from all but those individuals who, because of their own inner experience, have the sensitivity to become aware of it themselves.

Given your refined level of perception you will over time discover many a self-revelatory passage in my writings—revelations that I was obliged to provide but which I wrote in such an opaque way that only those who are inwardly developed to a high degree will be able to decipher what I meant. I must admit that at times I felt a mischievous delight in meeting my obligations but in a way that could be understood only by a very few who truly had earned the right. The form I use to cloak such passages is purposeful and will surely not disorient true spiritual seekers. My intention here is not to be secretive; it is simply a means to guard myself against foolish and distorted interpretations.

The seriousness of my motives will be apparent if you bear in mind that my eternal self—far removed from all earthly influences—is known to me as *timeless* and distinct from my earthly self. Yet I know that it is not at all supernatural since I have always been conscious of its eternal, spiritual nature as being my *own*. A problem arose only after a physical body was born for me in which to house my spiritual self and I entered the realm of time: It became imperative for my mortal self to become conscious of my eternal self—a task more important than the fulfillment of any earth-bound strivings of my physical being. Many decades were needed for this integration to complete itself. Again and again the earthly, human will to satisfy its own earthly desires stood in the way of my ability to completely realize an inner union with my timeless being. With a defiance that can at times lead to bizarre situations, the mortal human being insists on experiencing the fullness of its earthly existence and fears that it will be supplanted by something beyond the earth, something unfamiliar and unknowable, and so resists this integration. When viewed from an earthly point of view, this conflict is inevitable—a natural process that is inherent in such a task.

I did not expect these matters to come up so soon between us. I sense that it is your nature to seek answers yourself rather than asking a lot of questions and to face facts squarely right from the start—facts that cause others to stumble badly at times on their inner journey. I also sense that you are more in need of confirmation than help on your path and that you could almost do without even such confirmation.

It is evident that help from the radiant Spirit is near to you.

> Those still bound
> by self-importance
> will not find what they are looking for.
> Only those who cast the self away
> and bury their illusions
> will attain the inner gifts
> they so fervently desire.

LETTER SIX

WHAT ONE MUST LEAVE BEHIND

YOU SEEM SURPRISED THAT MANY OF THE questions you once had about my writings have resolved themselves as my words have gradually became clearer to you. I can only welcome your growing familiarity with my books—not because you have thus absolved me from giving many a demanding explanation but, first and foremost, for your own sake.

Only when you are able to answer a question for *yourself* has it been truly answered for you. Answers that come to you from without can, at best, point you in the right direction so that you may find the answer you seek. But it will still be up to you to make the answer *your own.* Every answer you receive from outside yourself that you have not understood from your inner experience and made your own will remain unresolved and give rise to even more questions.

As you read my books, you will come to see ever more clearly that my writings truly answer all questions that concern the eternal, spiritual nature of human beings—as best as the ability of the mind to understand such concepts permits. In doing so, however, I simply point out the *direction* to which the soul must turn if it wishes to find its *own* answers. Those who are honest with themselves will soon know whether a particular passage in my teachings is relevant to their individual situation or not. But they must not expect to find every possible shading of experience discussed in my writings—I simply describe the main elements.

I deliberately avoid interpreting concepts that derive from philosophical and theological theories in the usual ways because my teachings deal with the experience of *Reality*. This Reality, however, *begins* where philosophical and theological theories *end*—because these are theories that the seeking human spirit has created as *intellectual* paths to the eternal Spirit, which can only be known through *experience*. If those who are wedded to philosophical or theological concepts are to benefit from my writings, they must first outgrow their conviction that their beliefs have led them to the truth about Reality.

What I state here is not merely some assertion for which proof must be provided. Rather, I am informing you here of facts that you need to know right from the beginning of your journey—facts with which every one of my serious readers will eventually have to come to terms. One must first be done with one's philosophical and theological convictions before one can embark on the path to timeless Reality—a goal that will more easily be reached when one is burdened by fewer mental constructs.

You have probably already noticed in your first perusal of my writings the tolerance I extend towards every religious belief or intellectual opinion as long it reflects spiritual Reality, even if only in an attenuated way. But my tolerance should not lead anyone to assume that I am thereby suggesting that philosophical and theological thinking could be a path to timeless Reality. Rather, I respect such human endeavors when I sense that their motives are sincere and I honor whatever partial truths about eternal Reality have already been found in these approaches, or may be found in the future.

The only path, however, that leads into the everlasting, unchanging eternal Reality is a path of *becoming*—not merely of knowing. All of my books have been written to clearly mark out this path.

Blessings for your journey on the path upon which you have now embarked!

LETTER SEVEN

THE TEMPLE OF ETERNITY

YOU ASK WHETHER OTHER READERS OF my books have expressed thoughts similar to those you voiced in your last, most significant letter. The answer to your question is found in *The Book on the Living God,* in the chapter "The Tabernacle of God is with Men"—the very same chapter to which you referred at some length.

You have told me that since earliest youth you have felt within you a conviction that there exists a circle of men living in deep seclusion, unknown to the rest of the world, who send out blessings from their midst—and that you are somehow in connection with them. Because this conviction is so very important to you, let me comment a bit further on it. After *The Book on the Living God* was published, I began to receive reports, quite frequently, from others who also felt such a conviction, to some degree or another. These were people who did not show a proclivity toward fanciful daydreams; thus, it appears that you are in good and respectable company.

Concerning the place on earth where this sacred circle exists, you certainly are not as far off the mark as others who have told me that they believe it to be an Armenian monastery in the Caucasus, on some island in a peaceful ocean, or even in a huge cosmopolitan city. The fact that you imagine a "castle" on a very high mountain "in the midst of snow and ice" may mean that you are receiving a transmission of thought from this circle of men, and are thus able to see scenes familiar to them. They are the ones who know of a sacred, hidden sanctuary at a most auspicious location on earth. This sanctuary can only be perceived by human beings whose spiritual senses are awakened and thus able to discern forms made of spiritual substance. When viewed through the senses of the mortal body, one can only see earthly scenes made up of physical substance in this place—and one would be deceived into believing that nothing else exists here. It would be impossible for even the best photographic equipment, using the most sensitive film, to capture anything other than these physical forms.

The structure that exists at this site, made up of crystal-clear, eternal spiritual substance, cannot be perceived by the physical body—not even by those members of the small circle who live nearby, and whose presence you feel so clearly. All those who are allowed to enter do so in the spiritual form they assume within the spiritual dimension. This spiritual form corresponds to their true nature far more than does their physical form and is not subject to the limitations of the material world. In this Temple of Eternity on earth no cult is celebrated and no instructive sermons are given. Here the members of this small circle, chosen by the everlasting Spirit as true priests, unite in order to enter into a sublime state of absolute union with the Father. It is a process of transubstantiation that can only occur at this location, where the required spiritual conditions are present, and cannot occur anywhere else on earth. It is an absolute *unio mystica* beyond anything conceivable even by a mystic. In this luminous state of eternal love the members of this circle direct currents of blessings all over the planet to those who have made themselves ready to receive such blessings—and it is from this place alone that those who are ready to receive such blessings can be reached.

Your imagination has led you to a vision quite close to reality as this site of the Temple of Eternity on earth is, indeed, not at all unlike a castle on a high mountain in the midst of snow and ice.

One needs to distinguish, however, between the site of the spiritual Temple, visible only to the spiritual senses, and a place of residence, visible to the physical senses, where a few among those who belong to this circle live in community. This place of residence is not situated on a high mountain nor in the midst of snow and ice. For those members of the circle who live there, it is simply a home they have chosen, just as other human beings choose where they live.

Due to the nature of their spiritual calling, these members of the circle are required to live in utmost seclusion from the outside world. Their isolation is protected by others outside their circle so that they will never be forced to give up their seclusion, even if shallow Western "civilization" should intrude on them even more than it has up to now.

The connection you feel with this spiritual circle of whose existence you are quite certain is by no means self-deception. However, it is important that you understand how this connection comes about. Allow me to illustrate using two inventions from the field of the electro-technological transmission of sound waves, because I am concerned that you not cling to a false concept of how it occurs. The connection you feel is not like a telephone connection where a single individual speaks to a single listener. Rather, it is like a radio message that is broadcast at certain frequencies over the entire earth. Different "broadcasts" are sent out over many different "frequencies" but you will only receive the one to which you are "tuned in."

Whenever the Mediators of Eternal Light influence events on earth, their intervention is accomplished in a manner similar to the analogy given here, even when, in times past, entire peoples came under such influence. It is important to understand, however, that such influence—always and under all circumstances—only concerns matters of the eternal Spirit and never efforts to secure material welfare or struggles for the recognition of some political ideology.

No human striving or action can receive support from the realm of the eternal Spirit other than that which leads into eternal spiritual Reality—that very place from whence the help came. Only when the creative power of the individual is dedicated to an awakening in the radiant Spirit, only when the temporal power achieved by whole peoples and nations is dedicated purely to the power of the radiant Spirit—only then can individuals and nations come under the spiritual influence that emanates from the Temple of Eternity on this earth.

Please contemplate carefully everything I have said in this letter until, hopefully, I can soon pick up the thread again. May the light-filled blessings from the Temple of Eternity find you always ready to receive them.

LETTER EIGHT

ABOUT MY SPIRITUAL NATURE

YOUR RECENT LETTER HAS INSPIRED ME to answer in verse. The poems that follow will show you in succinct form that, guided by your own intuition, you have interpreted certain interrelationships, which I describe in my writings, correctly. However, when I refer to "we" in the first verse I am not speaking of the "royal we" but, rather, out of my eternal spiritual being that is always in seamless union with my brothers born of the Spirit and abiding in everlasting Light. In these verses I speak in spiritual unity with those of my spiritual brothers who, like myself, have been incarnated in a physical body in order to accomplish a particular task on this earth—a task determined by the Spirit and unique to each one of us.

I advise you to always pay close attention to the perspective from which I am writing in a given passage for, as the last stanza of the first verse says, I am a mortal human being indissolubly merged with my spiritual being.

WE

We are those called upon to be witnesses
for we live in eternal Light
Our testimony can never be altered
because we weigh with weights that are true

We are as we have been since time began
with the Father, in eternal Being
Yet we have been chosen by the Spirit
to be given a physical body and being
to be our "shrine" in the realm of Time

While still in the Spirit's realm
long before the earth began
we recognized the being who would become
our shrine
We were already merged with it
long before it became time-bound

We remain forever unified
with the mortal who here is our voice
melded together in the Light
tempered and purified by fire

Now that I have shown how my spiritual brothers and I are anchored in the realm of timeless Spirit, let me answer your questions that pertain to me personally.

I

I am not "I"
like those who use the word "I"
to refer to something that sets its own borders
like those who only accept their mortal nature
as real

I know myself as "I"
a being liberated in Light
The image and appearance of myself
lives in earthly limitation
and endures the torment and pain
born of the realm of Time

❧

There where I am is Eternity
because eternal space
pervades the earthly space
that fills my days here on earth

I gave myself to this mortal body
causing it suffering
exhausting its reserves
so that eternal space

may pervade it completely
so that the eternal
may reveal itself within it

❧

When I grant you the gift of highest good
chosen from the most sublime of costly
treasures
I do not merely offer you wise words
as if these word were a possession for me to
give away

What I give you
is and remains *my own*
even if I give to countless many
My words can show you the path and goal
to follow
because *I live* in every one of them

I think it would be correct to assume that what I have written here will not awaken new questions in you. Rather, I believe I may be answering in advance some questions that—reading between the lines of your welcome letter—you may be asking me in the near future. But here too you should not accept anything unless you have verified it for yourself. Only when your own eternal self willingly gives you its agreement will your doubts—some of which may as yet be hidden even from yourself—be truly and definitively answered and no longer able to jeopardize your progress on the path.

I hope I will soon be able to write to you about a number of things that you touched on in your letter just prior to this most recent one. But if some time should elapse before I am able to respond, I ask you in advance not to wait impatiently for mail to arrive. What I have yet to tell you about the Mediators of Eternal Light and the spiritual guidance and help they offer will still reach you in a timely fashion, and will not slow down your inner development, even if it should take me many months to answer.

I bless you and send you all the help you have need of on the path to your eternal self.

LETTER NINE

HOW SPIRITUAL HELP REACHES US

MY LAST LETTER, IN WHICH I USED rhythmic verse as the best way to express what I had to say, certainly did not call for an answer. Yet, I welcome your response, for it clearly issues from the depths of your soul and tells me that you have again understood everything exactly as I intended. However, I was surprised to learn that you are wondering from where your insights have come.

The insight and understanding you have come to truly did not stem from your "flesh and blood" but, rather, from your eternal self. Only through the eternal self can one come to know the truth about the Reality in which that eternal self dwells. The realizations of flesh and blood, that is, thinking and feeling that is limited by the constraints of the earthbound, animal-like existence, are related to the realizations that only our spiritual self can give us in the same way that the consciousness of an ordinary pebble lying in a stream is related to the highest forms of conscious life known to us. Knowledge of the Eternal can only reach the human being from out of the eternal realm.

Let me use this opportunity to also provide you with some clarification that should have been included in my earlier reply to your remarks on the chapter "The Tabernacle of God Is with Men" in *The Book on the Living God.* Unfortunately, circumstances forced me to end that letter before I could include everything I would have wanted to tell you.

When I described to you in a prior letter how the connection between souls here on earth and the Mediators of Eternal Light comes about, I used an analogy to two well-known and widely used inventions to illustrate my point.* What I did not spell out in that letter is already clearly explained in the chapter "The

---

* See Letter Seven: "The connection you feel is not like a telephone connection where a single individual speaks to a single listener. Rather, it is like a radio message that is broadcast at certain frequencies over the entire earth."

Spirit's Light Dwells in the East" from *The Book on the Living God.* When anyone misinterprets the explanations given there it can only mean that they have been inattentive in their reading. Again and again I receive letters from individuals who tell me, with an excited air of self-importance, about inner voices they have experienced, supposing them to be from a guiding "master"—a Mediator of Eternal Light. As a matter of precaution, so that you do not compare yourself to these people, I would like to direct your attention to what I *actually* say in the aforementioned chapter as well as in the chapter "The Inner Journey," which is the central chapter of *The Book on the Living God.*

One has to twist around the words I have written in these passages—and especially also in the book *Resurrection*—in order to come to an understanding completely contrary to all that I have actually said. It should be clear to any careful reader that I am not referring to the kinds of "inner voices" one might hear in states of ecstasy that are the result of an over-stimulated nervous system or by individuals with an overwhelming need to feel important. These inner voices are produced by a temporary or permanent split in the personality.

It is exactly these kinds of "voices" that I caution against in all my writings.

Surely, I may expect my readers to understand that I use the words "voice" and "speaking" metaphorically—as I have repeatedly made this point. I have clearly stated that this metaphorical "speaking" should by no means be compared to actual speaking of a human language. Instead, what I am describing is the experience of becoming clear about a concept that was previously unclear, through the intervention of a being who itself dwells in a state of absolute clarity. The fact that I have placed these words—which some seem to believe they can appropriate and use with a completely contrary meaning—in quotation marks should clearly indicate to any sensible reader that I want them to be understood in a figurative way. In the chapter "The Spirit's Light Dwells in the East" of *The Book on the Living God*, I also expressly say that what one hears within is "spoken" by a sacred voice that creates inner clarity directly, without the medium of human speech and not in any language spoken on this earth. Surely all I have said here is clear enough.

In the central chapter of *The Book on the Living God*, "The Inner Journey," I touch upon the *possibility* that a spiritual teacher may show himself to pupils who are to receive inner clarity in a non-material, "magical image" if they have the predisposition to receive help in this way. I mentioned this in order to describe everything that might happen when one is receiving inner clarification and left no room for any reader to think that this "image" might be the master himself. At the same time, I also clearly stated that a person predisposed to seeing this kind of image is in no way favored. But I could not fail to mention such a possibility in a book dealing with spiritual matters even though it occurs very rarely and depends upon the presence of certain conditions seldom found in a Westerner.

I know that you pay careful attention to each one of my words and so would never interpret them in these erroneous ways. But you may come across other readers of my books who will tell you about their "inner voices" with an air of mystery, in the false belief that I approve of these kinds of voices. On the contrary, these are *sinister* manifestations and *always and under all circumstances* constitute a threat to those who have not been trained to evaluate the reliability of spiritual phenomena by using their spiritual faculties of discernment. When dealing with these people, you need to be very sure of yourself and what you know and recognize that they are mostly slaves of their own fanaticism and conceit, obsessed with the delusion that they are receiving "higher guidance." Otherwise, you might give credence to such accounts and even let yourself be persuaded that you are not yet as advanced as these deluded believers. You might begin to worry that your "dry and sober disposition," as you describe it, is an obstacle to spiritual progress or brood over similar concerns about yourself that self-critical individuals often harbor.

In order to make sure that you are completely clear about everything, let me bring to your attention another misunderstanding that I truly never expected to encounter until, to my astonishment, I was forced to recognize how prevalent it actually is. One cannot help but wonder if the use of metaphors and similes—which are so essential when attempting to illustrate spiritual concepts—is no longer understood by today's readers, accustomed as they are to the matter-of-fact writing style used in newspaper reporting. Otherwise, it would not be possible for concepts such as "spiritual closeness," "sublime help," "spiritual guidance," or "spiritual protection" from those spiritual helpers empowered to offer these things to be misinterpreted to mean that a Mediator of Eternal Light actually has to be *physically* near those who need help or guidance in order for them to be able to experience this benevolent *spiritual* nearness.

The process I allude to when I use these and similar words in my books unfolds in a very different manner. I would expect rational individuals, capable of thinking logically, to realize this on their own. How could one be so befuddled as to suppose that the number of Mediators of Eternal Light here on earth, along with their spiritual brothers who have not been incarnated—all of whom are capable of offering spiritual help free from the limitations of the material world—would be large enough in proportion to the earth's population to personally approach all who require their help? Furthermore, would it not be disturbing to know that one is being observed at all times, without one's permission, by an invisible being who is also one's benevolent helper? Fortunately, there is nothing in the realm of Reality that in any way resembles this. The conviction by certain individuals that they are so important that the smallest details of their trivial, everyday concerns must be known in the realm of the Spirit and ought to be the subject of help from that realm is a delusion and completely untrue.

The help given by those Mediators of Eternal Light who are tasked with rendering such help relates solely to the human being's eternal spirit: that is, to spiritual distress, the need for spiritual protection, or the need for spiritual guidance. Those human beings who are beset by such difficulties will unfailingly be found by these helpers without them having even a vague idea of the physical location of the individual needing their help. It is a purely *spiritual* process that allows them to reach those in need with absolute certainty and at all times.

In my former letter, I used an analogy to telephone and radio transmission to describe how spiritual help is "broadcast." I would now like you to imagine—although this analogy is not perfect—an immense switchboard onto which the immeasurable vastness of space has been projected in microscopically reduced proportions. Imagine that each soul on earth is represented by two platinum electrodes occupying a tiny space on this board. The moment a soul is in need of spiritual guidance or help a bright spark is emitted by those two electrodes. A Mediator of Eternal Light empowered to help or guide is like an electrical engineer facing such a switchboard, on which there are also countless levers that activate different types of electrical currents. The color and variations in the frequency of the sparks will precisely indicate to him which current or combination of currents is required in order to render either help, protection or spiritual guidance, and he would immediately know which type of current to activate. Once that current is activated, spiritual help reaches the person in need automatically.

Sparks between the electrodes representing a particular human being will not be emitted unless such individuals fervently expect or request guidance, protection, or help from the realm of the living, radiant Spirit—and also not unless they have prepared themselves inwardly to be able to receive and make use of such help.

I don't think I need to tell you that no such switchboard made of spiritual substance actually exists. Rather, the image I have described here is meant to illustrate in symbolic form certain relationships that exist within the structure of timeless, spiritual life. May this analogy help you to gain a correct understanding of the way in which spiritual help, spiritual guidance, and spiritual protection take place.

The help and spiritual guidance offered by a Mediator of Eternal Light, and through him by our entire fellowship in the Spirit, never focuses on matters that begin and end between cradle and grave. Rather, such help is concerned solely with the awakening of the soul within the timeless spiritual realm and, if possible, during life on earth, so that the individual's mortal consciousness of the soul can carry over and unite with the timeless, spiritual self.

And with this, let me end this rather long letter and recommend that you read it with special care, so that its contents may be absorbed by your soul.

May my blessings, which will reach you in the very same way as I have described in this letter, clearly illuminate your insight into all matters that flow from the eternal realm.

LETTER TEN

GOD IS NOT INVOLVED IN WORLD AFFAIRS

I WAS DELIGHTED TO HEAR THAT YOU FULLY understood the explanation I wrote in my last letter, describing how spiritual help and guidance is remotely transmitted by those who are able to offer such guidance and help because they have been empowered to do so by the eternal Spirit. But now, in your new letter, I notice that you express uneasiness each time you encounter, in my writings, the idea that entire peoples have been influenced by the spiritual reach of the Mediators of Eternal Light.

Here it may be useful for me to point out once again that *all* spiritual help for which the eternal Father, dwelling in the Light of the Beginning, employs the Mediators of Eternal Light, who through their union with Him dwell in the same Light, can always only reach individual souls. Thus, entire peoples can only be subject to this spiritual influence insofar as there are enough individuals within a people who have "sculpted" their souls into a form that is ready to receive and understand that help—so that spiritual guidance and help will find hearts ready to absorb it. There exists no other kind of spiritual help or guidance for human beings on earth.

In my last letter to you I described how spiritual influence is concerned only with helping the human soul to reawaken to the consciousness of its eternal nature, while leaving matters of this temporal world—the life between cradle and grave—completely up to humans themselves. Despite what I have said, it seems from your latest letter as if some inner longings, possibly inherited or acquired, cause you to hope against hope that there may, after all, be some kind of spiritual influence on world affairs.

It is always a mistake to believe that the eternal, divine Father may, at some place or time, be involved—either directly or by sending spiritual guidance to human beings—in the internal or external politics of peoples or nations. Likewise, the belief that the outcomes of the severe crises of political entities, known as "wars" and "revolutions," reflect the eternal will of the Spirit simply reveals how frightfully ignorant human beings are of matters concerning the spirit and soul.

It is only animal-bound human beings who are active participants in these world crises. The factors that spur them into action, including the incitement by sinister influences originating from the invisible part of the physical world, are purely terrestrial in nature and are not at all subject to spiritual influences and forces.

> You say:
> The history of the world
> is its own judgment.
> True enough—
> but it is humanity itself
> that pronounces the verdict upon itself.
> Here the "Almighty"
> has relinquished its power
> and only the voice of animal-enslaved life
> cut off and far from the Spirit's life
> is heard.

The only thing that can create a better lot for humanity in its days between cradle and grave is the awakening of many individual souls to their eternal selves. However, there will always only be subgroups of humanity in which there are enough spiritually awakened individual souls who will be able to live life in a way that is worthy of the Eternal that dwells within the human being. Through their example, they will gradually be able to wrest other subgroups away from their enslavement to their animal nature. One part of humanity will someday give birth to children who will already have awakened to the Spirit while in their mothers' wombs. Another part, hopelessly bound to their animal nature, will sire children who are quite the opposite: not the "super-men" envisioned by Friedrich Nietzsche* but, rather, super-animals who will exceed every other animal in dullness, cruelty, and killer-instinct—to the point of self-destruction.

---

* Friedrich Nietzsche (1844-1900) was a German philosopher who developed the concept of the *Übermensch,* or super-man. In his 1883 book, *Thus Spake Zarathustra*, he set forth the idea of a new generation of superior men, or *Übermenschen,* who will use their will to achieve the ultimate in human potential while on earth, for the good of all humanity.

That is all that I wish to say to you today and I hope that, in the future, you will not be enticed by wishful daydreams into believing that the "finger of God" is at work in world affairs.

May the blessings of the Spirit's Light be with you always.

LETTER ELEVEN

HOW GOD GRANTS HELP TO INDIVIDUALS

I CAN WELL UNDERSTAND THAT IT HAS NOT been easy for you to adjust your worldview over the last few months in accordance with the points I raised in my last letter. I can empathize with you because some decades ago I too had difficulty letting go of everything I had heard and readily believed since childhood, when for the first time I was confronted with reality.

For this reason, I am all the more happy to hear that you now feel yourself liberated from a heavy and paralyzing weight which, even in your happiest hours, had never left you. After all, it is hardly tolerable to believe that eternal benevolence and love reigns with unlimited power over this planet and yet still calmly allows all that is terrible, frightful, and loathsome to take place day after day and night after night—even though it would seem that these blights could be so easily prevented by divine intervention. Such a belief can certainly oppress the soul. It is understandable that one would breathe a sigh of relief once one has arrived at the insight that this notion has no grounding in reality but is merely the result of a false concept of God created by a distressed humanity that has distanced itself from the truth of the divine.

You would be quite mistaken, however, to interpret my words as meaning that I regard matters between cradle and grave as unimportant. These things are of great importance to me because they continue to have consequences that last beyond their own time—even if these consequences do not necessarily last for all eternity. But even in the immediate, it is of utmost importance that we treat the matters of everyday life with care and respect their importance.

You would also be seriously mistaken if you concluded that I am saying that no divine influence exists at all with regard to our lives on earth. Not only is such influence possible but it is in fact a frequent, even a daily, occurrence. This happens spontaneously through the powers and forces radiating from the realm of the Spirit, when a human being on earth acts in ways that conform to spiritual law—without that person doing anything beyond this to bring about that help. Many religious precepts and even many superstitious maxims have their origin in this truth. This is because, throughout time, people have noticed that those who act in accordance with spiritual laws bring good things to themselves and those who violate these laws cause themselves to suffer. We see this connection between right and wrong behavior and receiving or not receiving divine help described in some ancient religious teachings—including in the Psalms of David where it is vividly dramatized through the use of personification and other poetic devices. In these accounts, those who act in accordance with eternal laws are favored by God and find that many a good and pleasant thing manifests in their earthly lives. Those who violate eternal laws are seen as despising God and are portrayed as "fools" and "blasphemers"—victims of their own willfulness or ignorance, when they could easily have learned a better way. If one considers these testimonies from past human history, one might be astonished at the wisdom gleaned in what many people today regard as a somewhat barbaric time. One might well ask if we contemporary Europeans are not worse barbarians than any prior generation might have been.*

To be sure, we have acquired knowledge that these ancients did not possess. But I doubt that these peoples of ages past would have wanted to exchange their folk wisdom, gained through millennia of experience, with the body of knowledge that we today accept as true but which has not withstood the test of time. One has only to read the Psalms of the Old Testament at face value, without considering how they were used to justify religious dogma, to become convinced of how

* The German-language original of this book was published in 1935, at a time when Germany was fast descending into a night of barbarism under Nazi rule. The antisemitic and racist Nuremberg Laws were passed at that time. Books written by Jews and political opponents of the Nazis were being burned during huge public rallies. Much more was to come. It would have been clear to any reader at the time that Bô Yin Râ was making a thinly veiled, ironic reference to Germany. He may also have had in mind the brutality of WW1. We can also assume that Bô Yin Râ did not want to be more explicit because that would have caused his books to be banned by the Nazi regime and thus become unavailable to his readers—a fate they ultimately did not escape.

deeply their authors—writing under cover of the name of King David—penetrated into the mysteries of these automatically-released spiritual forces and powers. Of course, in doing so, one must disregard all the ritualistic uses to which the Psalms were put, which are irrelevant to their essential content. One should also not be misled by the fact that the workings of these spiritual forces and powers are described, not as immutable law but, rather, as being subject to the whims of godly emotions. It is possible that the authors themselves still believed in this interpretation—but it is more likely that they thought it necessary in order to hide the truth of how these laws actually work. Because human beings of that time were only able to conceive of God as a capricious, power-hungry ruler—a projection of their own human qualities—the authors of the Psalms might have thought that the truth would throw people into a state of confusion and even lead them to doubt the existence of God at all.

There is much wisdom whose true "face" was once plainly recognizable but whose intended meaning has been distorted through centuries of misuse because it has been viewed through the lens of preconceived religious beliefs. It takes a sharp eye and considerable effort to discover the original outlines of what were once easily discernable contours.

If my words inspire you to practice your own ability to correctly discern and interpret such blurred and garbled passages in the accounts of the distant past, then many joys of discovery await you.

May the blessings emanating from Light everlasting reach you at all times.

LETTER TWELVE

THE FORCES OF THE SOUL

IT DID NOT COME AS A SURPRISE TO ME that you have the impression, as do many other of my readers, that it must be nearly impossible to unite the forces of the soul within oneself. This feeling has its basis in what I have written about soul forces in *The Book on the Living God*, in the chapter "On Death," and elsewhere. No other passage in my books has caused such an abundance of questions and requests for clarification from my readers to land on my desk.

But I must tell you that all worry about the difficulty which does in truth exist with respect to unifying the soul forces is the result of a misconception concerning the nature of these forces. It is no different in your case.

Because I have received so many inquiries, I once again reviewed everything I have written in various places about the necessity of unifying the soul forces within oneself. I looked at these passages and reviewed my wording in the spirit of scrupulous self-examination and willingness to be critical of my explanations. Even so, I was not able to fault myself for the mistaken impressions of some readers nor could I discover any word that I would have wanted to be different.

I had to, of course, point out in these passages that a considerable degree of self-discipline is necessary in order to undertake the task of unifying the soul forces within one's self. When I say in the passages to which you referred that it is easier to "hold a raging elephant by no more than a string of hemp and guide him through a market's busy crowd than fully to unite, within a single human will, the countless wills that form a human soul," I also point out that this "miracle" can nevertheless occur. Indeed, it *must* occur if a soul is to be ready to receive its Living God within. This is difficult to achieve—but not impossible! It might be of interest to you to know that I especially enjoyed using the analogy to a raging elephant because it was one that my former spiritual teacher liked to use in conversations with me—an image drawn from the world familiar to him.

Any individual of sound mind is capable of surmounting the difficulties involved in unifying the soul forces. Indeed, those with only the most rudimentary schooling may be more able to overcome the obstacles involved than many highly educated, intellectual persons as the latter may be unable to summon the energy and endurance essential for the task.

Bear in mind that I am not recommending some sort of method for reaching this goal. Instead, my texts are a serious body of teachings in which I seek to inform those humans whose souls long for the Light about the structure of timeless, spiritual life, in a way that can be comprehended by them. For this reason, I had to discuss everything that has ever been and always will be possible for human beings on earth to experience within the life of the radiant Spirit. But not everything is possible for everyone. By referring to my books, seekers can determine what is possible for themselves. To be sure, inherited psychophysical traits play a part but, in the main, energy and perseverance will determine what those who seek their eternal self can achieve during life on earth. Just as one can become a successful merchant without having a special talent for arithmetic, it is possible to attain a full experience of one's eternal self by resolutely persevering on the spiritual path, even if one lacks the innate aptitude for making progress on this journey. To be sure, one must dedicate one's entire inner and outer life to this purpose. In doing so, it is of the greatest importance where one seeks one's pleasures because nothing has a stronger impact on the soul than the objects, activities, and events that give us pleasure.

But now let me speak to the misconception concerning the actual nature of the soul forces mentioned at the beginning of this letter.

Over time, I have noted a curious similarity in the ideas my readers have formed about soul forces. Again and again I have encountered the view that soul forces are something similar to our bodily senses, easily and clearly distinguishable in the way the sense of sight may be distinguished from the sense of sound or smell. This view, however, does not in any way correspond to reality. Although it is not incorrect to say that our character traits—that is, the way we act and feel with the help of the senses and their readiness to react—are determined by the soul forces, the soul forces cannot be as clearly differentiated from each other as can the physical senses. Rather, one may compare the soul forces to the nerve cells of the body—indeed to the nervous system as a whole. Every nerve has its specific function and yet is part of a network of countless other nerves giving rise to manifold interactions. Similarly, each soul force—even if one is unable to give it a specific name—has its spiritually determined function while also being in constant interaction with all other soul forces which make up a soul and may, under special circumstances, have an effect far beyond the soul that encompasses it.

The union of the soul forces under a single ordering will would be an impossible undertaking if it were necessary to first give each one a specific name—that is, to form an exact idea as to the nature and function of each individual soul force. Fortunately, our eternal self never makes demands on us that cannot be met, nor would such knowledge about each individual soul force, no matter how detailed, bring one any closer to the goal. The union of the soul forces is exclusively a matter of aligning one's will with the clear intent to rule and order them.

The challenge here is to maintain this intent of will without deviation for even a single, conscious second, regardless of what temptations the outside world may offer.

This is the greatest challenge that must be mastered on the path to God. Nevertheless, it *can* be mastered—and countless seekers have succeeded in doing so over the course of human history. Identical to this task is the shaping of one's eternal self, of which I spoke in an earlier letter, and in this endeavor life on earth in a physical body serves as a workshop. I teach my readers to view these matters from multiple perspectives so that they can fathom the reality that I try to show in words.

I hope that this letter has reassured you and eased your worry that more is being required of you than you are able to master. Right now you are still in your "workshop" and are able, with the tools offered to you, to shape the quality and richness of your eternal self. Once you have left your mortal body, your ability to shape your eternal self ends. Let us hope that by then you will have formed your eternal self to reflect what you now hope to achieve.

May blessings flow to you from Light everlasting.

LETTER THIRTEEN

ON NEW EDITIONS OF MY BOOKS

GOETHE'S FIVE-ACT DRAMA *UR-GÖTZ** was originally meant to be read, but not performed. Goethe later adapted it for the stage and a well-intentioned friend suggested that he show this stage version to a prominent elderly nobleman who had already expressed great delight in the original version. This man, according to Goethe, identified with the

---

* *Urgötz oder Die Geschichte Gottfriedens von Berlichingen mit der eisernen Hand dramatisiert* is a drama in five acts written in 1771 and intended to be read rather than performed. Goethe wrote a shortened version specifically for performance entitled *Götz von Berlichingen,* in full *Götz von Berlichingen mit der eisernen Hand* (*The Dramatized Story of Gottfried von Berlichingen with the Iron Hand*), which was published in 1773 and performed in 1774. The play was based on the memoirs of a Franconian knight, adventurer, and poet who lived from 1480-1562 and did battle with various feudal governments. Through Götz's story, Goethe was able to make oblique criticisms of contemporary political tyranny.

play's brave old hero. Goethe firmly rejected his friend's suggestion. He argued that the admirer of the first version would certainly be disappointed to see that much had been omitted, reorganized, and treated in a completely different manner in the revised version.

Your welcome letter immediately reminded me of Goethe's psychologically sound, wise refusal. In it you informed me that you had read the earlier editions of those of my books that I recently carefully revised and that you had only now heard about these final editions with their expanded texts. You say, quite understandably, that you have "become so used to certain parts of the older versions" that, despite the fact that you "agree with the newer and much clearer versions," you still regret to see that those cherished parts were changed. The first versions were also dear to me, otherwise I would have never offered them to the public—although at the time the amiable and bustling head of the large publishing house that brought out these first versions almost literally tore the manuscripts out of my hands, leaving me little opportunity for final revisions. In the case of one of the books, the postman even brought me the finished book while I was barely expecting to receive the first proof!

Letting go of the earlier versions was difficult because, like the final versions, their form is the result of a faithful adherence to laws governing the spiritual effect of the sound of words. However, every revision I made in the original versions in favor of the current, definitive ones had a reason. Because of the rush to publish my manuscripts, many typographical errors had inevitably occurred—errors that at times even changed the meaning of an important passage into its opposite. In addition, a number of expressions influenced by my Franconian dialect needed to be changed as they were inappropriate in an instructional book on spiritual matters. Furthermore, as a result of various letters I have received and conversations I have had, I became aware of some passages where different wording seemed desirable or even necessary for the sake of clarity.

I was aware that the revision of a book already available to the public is a thankless task. However, I could not allow this to keep me from doing what was necessary. I was happily surprised to nevertheless receive many letters of thanks from readers who told me, again and again, how enthusiastically they welcomed these revised editions. I was aware that readers might have difficulties getting used to the unfamiliar revised editions and so this enthusiastic approval came as a surprise. You stand quite alone in your elegiac grief over the loss of certain passages that have now taken their final, though different, form. In fact, the only comment similar to yours was from a friend whose native language is not German. I certainly did not do him a service since he was confronted with different German words in passages that he had formerly understood but now had to labor over.

I hope that from now on you will turn only to the revised editions of the books in question and that you will come to realize ever more clearly that these revisions were absolutely necessary. They certainly were not done out of some whim or for esthetic reasons or because of the need to publish a reprint. Books of instruction such as I write are not to be revised unless the writer's responsibility towards the reader unequivocally demands that a revision is needed. To be sure, the better is always the enemy of the good. But that must not mislead one into foregoing the better in order to preserve the good.

May heaven bless you!

LETTER FOURTEEN

POLYTHEISM AND THE VENERATION OF SAINTS

YOU ARE CERTAINLY ON THE TRAIL OF truth when you suspect that some beliefs that were alive in the ancient polytheistic religions, as well as the veneration of saints found in Asian religious forms and Byzantine and Roman Christendom, have a solid foundation in that they are based on the existence of the Mediators of Primordial Light.

However, you would be quite wrong to suppose that these venerated figures, as they have been portrayed in legend, can be traced back to specific Mediators, or that the canonizations of such individuals by the Roman Catholic Church were the result of a secret knowledge of such relationships. I say this so that there will not be any misunderstanding in my support of your opinion.

The fact that there are women among these figures of veneration, whereas a Luminary can only appear on earth in a masculine body, does not disprove your supposition.

In the realm of the Spirit every Mediator, despite the masculinity of his perishable earthly body, is also inseparably united with the eternal Feminine and therefore he would be capable of giving expression to the world of Spirit as it manifests both through male and female polarities.

Among the treasury of concepts of ancient polytheistic religions as well as in various sacred cults, there exist individuals—including those figures who bear the distinction of having been declared to be holy by some earthly power—who may indeed have been Mediators of Primordial Light. But even if it were possible to prove such a lineage with the best of evidence one would still be far from understanding how the process of receiving help from them—that you intuitively sense—actually unfolds. That is, one would still not understand how appealing to a figure who has come down to us through legend and the need to venerate another, whether that figure is conceived of as purely heavenly or as a departed human being, invokes the helping spiritual power and blessings of the Mediators of Primordial Light. These Mediators are the sole source and only Reality from which the desired help and blessings flow.

It matters not what name the faithful give to the helper they call upon or how they explain to themselves the way in which the help is granted—these things have no bearing on what actually transpires. The help that comes to seeking souls is transmitted by a process analogous to the switchboard filled with electrodes of which I spoke in an earlier letter to you.* What happens when a supplicant prays to a venerated figure is not so very different from this analogy and any variations in the process are determined solely by the receptivity and conceptual world of the person seeking help.

For many if not all of these supplicants, given the state of their soul and their receptivity at the time, the power of their plea can be greatly intensified by visualizing their figure of veneration in as much detail as possible.

* See Letter Nine pages 66–68.

For instance, the following is said of Saint Anthony of Padua, whom the populace had already regarded as if canonized even before the Catholic Pope bestowed this honor on him posthumously:

> For whatever one may plead
> Saint Anthony, rich in wonders
> shall grant to those in need.
> Poverty, leprosy, confusion's night
> hell itself must yield to his might!
> He calms the ocean's tumultuous tide
> recovers lost treasures in his stride.
> The strong chain is cut in twain
> the diseased limb released from pain!
> Whoever calls on him young or old
> finds solace and relief tenfold.

The above folk prayer is a typical example of how the clear visualization of a venerated personage can bestow strength and confidence on the petitioner. You may perhaps know that Saint Anthony of Padua was a powerful, captivating preacher—a Portuguese monk who, after many journeys to preach the faith, finally died in Padua. He should not be confused with the hermit Saint Anthony of the Desert. This error was committed by Wilhelm Busch—who was not all that familiar with the

Church's holy figures—in his satire of Saint Anthony of Padua.*

What is important for petitioners is that they *feel* the promised solace and relief. Although the help they receive flows from the community of sublime helpers, the petitioners would in all likelihood not be able to imbue their plea with the needed power, and to then be open to receiving the sought-for help, without visualizing some figure to whom helping powers have been ascribed through legend or history. One must therefore allow them the use of this sort of aid for the needed visualization.

This process is similar to the modifications figures of veneration have often undergone over time and in different places. Apollo, Aphrodite, Artemis, and other deities of the ancient world were venerated in different locales and each locale endowed them with different attributes. In the same way, the "Mother of God" is now revered in countless places of pilgrimage, and each place of

---

* Wilhelm Busch (1832–1908) was a German humorist, poet, illustrator, and painter. He often satirized religious piety. The reference here is to his illustrated story "*Der Heilige Antonius von Padua.*"

worship emphasizes a particular aspect of her being that kindles the believers' confidence. I am referring here to the object of veneration who has evolved out of the sublime cult of Hagia Sophia, or divine wisdom—the epitome of the eternal Feminine, later associated with the Mother of Jesus. The fact that supplicants make pilgrimages to different places of Madonna-worship depending on their particular concern is not at all absurd—although it may appear so from the superficial point of view of those who deem themselves superior to such things. We are not dealing here with some crude and idolatrous replication of a beloved figure of worship, or with an excess of faith. Instead, we are dealing with the different energies and visual and legendary influences associated with various locales and the way in which the resonance between these energies and the psychological needs of the supplicants heightens the intensity of their prayer.

It is this intensity that determines if a prayer is to be "heard" in the realm of the radiant, eternal Spirit by those who have been designated to direct the energies of spiritual help to those in need. As long as the prayer of the supplicant reaches the realm of the Spirit with enough resonance, these helpers will answer the call, regardless of whether it comes from a pious Buddhist of the Mahayana school or from an individual steeped in the belief system of some other religion.

I urge you to make the disclosures I have given you today completely your own and then, using your own abilities, you will be able to discover even more.

Blessings to you from the realm of Light Everlasting!

LETTER FIFTEEN

THE NATURE OF LIFE IN THE LIGHT

THIS IS NOT THE FIRST TIME THAT SOMEone has written to me saying that through my writings, even without any further inner development, much that in the past had raised difficult questions has suddenly become clear and comprehensible—or, to use your words, "everything has received a fresh face."

This is not surprising since I am not writing about something that I "dreamed up" or discovered as a result of an intellectual process. Rather, I describe the structure of life within the eternal Spirit. I am able to do this because I am familiar with this life *from my own Light-filled experience*—more so than everything I have experienced outside of it. All life proceeds from the realm of radiant Spirit and, despite the fact that the clarity of our mortal consciousness is clouded by our animal nature, the brain nevertheless continuously receives influences issuing from this realm—regardless of whether it can discern them or whether it is too dull to do so. Thus, simply pointing out the structure of life in the realm of eternal Spirit can lead to an embryonic awakening after which the world will no doubt look a little different.

Whether such an awakening will give individuals all that they desire for their soul or whether they are now motivated to work towards ever higher levels of awakening will depend solely on them. However, whether or not the conditions in their external life will permit such work is not always under their control.

Many individuals who truly want to deepen their souls' awakening lack the strength to clear away all the earthly obstacles that prevent this. Others may have the needed strength but cannot allow themselves to eliminate these obstacles because doing so would prevent them from fulfilling important commitments. It would certainly not be right for human beings to simply leave undone things that they might well bring to completion or at least relative completion in this life on earth in order to devote themselves exclusively to their inner path. Those who neglect their earthly obligations will find themselves blocked from reaping the benefits of their efforts to develop on the inner path. Seekers will do well to be satisfied with what their earthly circumstances allow them to accomplish in the realm of the Spirit. All attempts to reach beyond what external circumstances allow must necessarily come to naught and may even endanger whatever treasures could have been added to their spiritual storehouse.

It is the same here as with everyday things: Those who ask for too much achieve very little. One should not move on to algebra and integral calculus if one has not yet mastered basic multiplication.

Many of those who seek to awaken within harbor the most fantastical ideas of what constitutes attainment within the realm of the Spirit. No amount of guidance can dissuade them from focusing on developing unusual capabilities within the *physical* self and seeking out the most extreme sensations instead of pursuing the experience of being alive in the Spirit. All physical sensations and experiences, no matter how wondrous, will necessarily be extinguished with the death of the mortal body. Many believe that they have had a spiritual experience when, in reality, all they have done is over-stimulate their nervous system. By amplifying sensations that are, when practiced in moderation, soul-enriching and healthful for the physical body, they create an artificial feeling of exaltation. Many seekers still consider this "spiritualization" of the body to be a necessary and noble aim—not understanding that its pursuit will only lead them from one self-deception to another. Only those few who seek *Reality*—and nothing else—and who avoid the lure of extreme sensation can reach the goal: to experience the world of the Spirit by *embodying the Spirit* while here on earth. This is the path set forth by the Spirit's law.

The person who understands with the mind
and is bound to earthly things
finds it difficult to understand
that in the eternal realm
that which is experienced
is not apart from the one who experiences.
For those who live in the eternal realm
only oneness exists.
Nothing is outside themselves

as is the case in life on earth
where experience and experiencer are two.

Seen from the eternal realm
mortal experience
is nothing but vapor and illusion.
Only that experience which unfolds
  with no effort
and requires no explanation
can open the space of the Eternal.

When Paul, the tentmaker from Tarsus, dares to proclaim: "Eye hath not seen, nor ear heard, neither have entered into the heart of man, the things which God hath prepared for them that love him" (1 Corinthians 2:9 KJV) he is describing in the clearest possible way the nature of true spiritual experience. Yet, the meaning of these words of wisdom has been misinterpreted and even reversed, suggesting that "the things which God hath prepared" for those who are God-loving refers to a feast for the senses, surpassing in the spiritual realm anything that may be experienced in the physical realm. Paul was a giant among those first individuals from Asia Minor to directly receive and personally experience the teachings of Jesus. Only by approaching him with respectful reverence and realizing how far removed his consciousness and world was from our own can we today understand him.

In the realm of Light
those who perceive
are one with perception and the thing
  perceived
What on earth appears as separate
is no longer apart in space and time
In the eternal realm
all things transpire at once
and in the same place

Unknowable to the mind
no words can describe these mysteries
No language can illuminate
what only life within the Light can
  understand

I hardly need to tell you that it would be my fondest wish to see you living the luminous life of the Spirit already here on earth.

The help that I send you through my blessings will always support your striving.

LETTER SIXTEEN

TRUE AWAKENING IS ALWAYS GENTLE

I DID NOT EXPECT THAT MY MENTION OF the Apostle Paul in my last letter would have led you to puzzle over his supposed sudden conversion from persecuting early Christians as a committed Pharisee to becoming a follower of Jesus. As you know from my book, *The Secret*, Paul was predestined to become a pupil of the Luminaries of Eternal Light and, because of this, found his way to an understanding of the true teachings of Jesus. In that book I explained that the entire Damascus story* must be understood allegorically—as a parable that describes a far less spectacular

* According to Biblical accounts, Paul's sudden conversion took place while he was traveling on the road to Damascus. The conversion is referred to in several of the Pauline Epistles, but the most dramatic account is told as a third person narrative in Acts 9:3-9.

event—if one would glimpse the kernel of truth embedded in it.

I refer you to what is written in *The Secret* so as not to have to repeat it here. However, in order to rule out any misinterpretation of what I wrote in that book, let me clearly state the following: The "sudden" transformation of this fanatical enemy of the teaching of Jesus into its most powerful and influential exegete was actually the result of a *gradual awakening* that Paul, in his tenacious quest for truth, struggled mightily to attain. Having reached these insights, Paul then resolved and strove to atone for his former wrongs, even though his intentions had been honorable.

If someone relates to you accounts of sudden, spontaneous awakenings or if you come across the like in old stories, you will do well to be skeptical. You should ask yourself whether you are dealing with an experience of spiritual Reality or something much more mundane.

Take for example the case of the unfortunate scholar, scientist, and inventor Emanuel Swedenborg, a man of many interests and talents who also enjoyed eating well and copiously. According to his own report, while eating a meal one evening, a man suddenly appeared seated near him. He heard the man shout: "Don't eat so much!" and then the man vanished into thin air. Regrettably, this incident had the effect of awakening Swedenborg's latent abilities as a medium. He then began to experience the strangest "heavenly insights" intermixed with scraps of science and to engage in extensive communications with what he assumed were heavenly spirits.

True awakenings in the realm of the eternal, radiant Spirit are never startling and abrupt. Instead, they take place slowly, step-by-step, each step following naturally from the one before, with a gradual increase in one's degree of inner awakening. Should you ever have an experience that feels to you like a "sudden awakening"—perhaps as a result of overwork or overwrought nerves—then you should immediately consult a *doctor* and, if possible, someone who is knowledgeable about the brain but also does not close the door to interpretations that don't fit into the accepted scientific framework of the day.

Such "awakenings" are by no means harmless and can lead to the splitting off of aspects of the self and a resultant fracturing of one's sense of self. The best safeguard against them is to calmly and serenely reject any sort of impatience as one progresses along the path to attaining consciousness within the Spirit. If you live by the general advice I give all readers in my books and also heed those words you feel were written especially for you, then your gradual awakening will be guided from a central place by the Luminaries of Eternal Light and will unfold in the way that is best for you.

Follow the path before you and calmly continue the journey that you have now begun in a manner that I find most encouraging. That path has been clearly marked and, through my writings, you will be able to recognize all the signposts that will lead you safely to your goal. But trust your own inner spiritual guidance—now that you understand how such guidance is given—to know what can be shown to you now as you travel on the path and what you may only expect at a later time. And do not forget that progressing on your path is not about acquiring new knowledge but, rather, about a process of *becoming* that will lead, over time, to a new and different sense of yourself as you go through your everyday life—a gradual transformation that in the end will enable you to consciously experience the Eternal within your own being.

May sublime help accompany you at all times on your path.

LETTER SEVENTEEN

JACOB BÖHME AND THE GERMAN MYSTICS

JACOB BÖHME WAS CERTAINLY MORE THAN just the "shoemaker of Görlitz," as people of questionable discernment are wont to describe him. He was not a shoemaker who was *also* a poet. All these trite allusions to the trade by which he earned his bread, which indeed did not require a high level of education, do not give a true picture of who Böhme was. In the small collection of individual essays published in the book *Signposts Along the Way* I pointed out, as you correctly understood, that Jacob Böhme had been accepted by the Luminaries of Eternal Light as one of their pupils. He considered this relationship to be so sacred that he shrouded it in secrecy. Although a great deal has been written about Böhme, no one has been in a position to fully understand this spiritual relationship and to describe it in a manner that does it justice.

To be sure, Jacob Böhme presents his spiritual experiences and insights in a rather baroque and idiosyncratic way, which is made even more convoluted through the wrong use of Latin and "Latinized" German words that he picked up from his learned friends. Those wishing to comprehend what he tried to convey must therefore have a clear understanding themselves of the nature of such experiences.

Things are quite different when it comes to understanding German mystics such as the anonymous author of the *Theologia Germanica,** Johannes Tauler,** Heinrich

---

* The *Theologia Germanica* is a mystical treatise believed to have been written in the late Fourteenth Century. It proposed that God and humankind can be united by pursuing a path of perfection, as exemplified by the life of Jesus. Martin Luther was an admirer of the book. It is notable for using German as a valid language for expressing theological ideas. The anonymous author was a member of the Teutonic Order, a Catholic religious order originally founded during the Crusades, and he lived in Frankfurt.

** Johannes Tauler (1300–1361) was a Dominican Catholic priest and a German mystic who was a disciple of Meister Eckhart. He taught that the state of the soul is affected more by a personal relationship with God than by external practices.

Seuse,* and Meister Eckhart. These were highly learned men who had arrived at their insights through rigorous philosophical analysis and who were saved from condemnation by the Catholic Church only with difficulty.

The story is opposite for the learned poet Johann Scheffler, who wrote under the name Angelus Silesius. Scheffler ultimately saved himself from the wrath of Lutheran church authorities by converting to Catholicism. In his writings, Scheffler transformed Catholic teachings by interpreting them in a symbolic and poetic manner.**

Another figure who needs to be considered quite apart from all the rest is the canon

---

* Heinrich Seuse (1295-1366) was also known as Heinrich von Suso, Heinrich Suss, and Heinrich von Berg. Seuse was a German Dominican friar, mystic, and noted author of the time. He was also notable for defending Meister Eckhart's legacy after Eckhart was posthumously condemned for heresy by the Catholic Church in 1329. Seuse was beatified by the Catholic Church in 1831.

** Johann Scheffler (1624-1677) was a German Catholic priest, physician, and poet who was influenced by the medieval German mystics and the work of Jakob Böhme. He was born and raised as a Lutheran but his mystical beliefs caused tension between him and Lutheran authorities. He converted to Catholicism in 1653.

regular Thomas à Kempis.* He was a pious person in the truest sense of the word. The four books that comprise his seminal text, *The Imitation of Christ*, though written from a completely Catholic point of view, are imbued with a soothing, benevolent spirit.

One can find occasional passages in the writings of the medieval German mystics that lead one to suppose they had some idea of the hidden existence of the Luminaries of Primordial Light. However, these men were not fully conscious of being in relationship with the Luminaries.

From what I once told you about the nature of spiritual help, it follows that they received spiritual help and guidance from this source—whether or not they were aware of its existence. One can clearly see this influence in the sermons and writings of Johannes Tauler, Heinrich Seuse, and Meister Eckhart, as soon as one clears away certain professions

* Thomas à Kempis (1380–1471) is best known as the author of *The Imitation of Christ*, one of the most widely read Christian devotional books. In Catholicism, a canon is a cleric who is attached to a cathedral. A "canon regular" is one who has taken monastic vows and lives in a monastic community. These terms are rarely used these days.

of faith and dogma. These churchly garments—that fit so poorly with the intent of these writings—were draped over the shoulders of their words in order to save the authors from being burned at the stake. Also, in the writings of Angelus Silesius, who should be considered mainly a mystical poet, and those of Thomas à Kempis, the spiritual influence of the Luminaries of Primordial Light can be seen in many places.

Despite my high regard for these medieval German mystical theologians and philosophers—despite my deep appreciation for the quiet and subtle Thomas à Kempis and my great delight in the exquisitely concise and at times polemical Angelus Silesius—you would be well advised to wait with the study of any mystical texts until you feel sufficiently secure on your path such that the occasional exploration of some byway will be unlikely to divert you from your goal.

I give you this advice so that you will not tarry too long on your path and spend time evaluating the merits of these mystics. Judgments that might take you a long time now will come to you later on without effort, and will not take time away from other endeavors that would bring you closer to your goal. Also, do not forget that the writings of all those I have just mentioned—with the sole exception of Jacob Böhme—are the products of the writers' personal views about the world of the eternal Spirit, gained through arduous mental labor and often intense emotional experiences. You, on the other hand, enjoy the unfathomably good fortune of having been shown the beginning of the path to eternal Reality at the very outset of your endeavors.

May you receive all the blessings of genuine spiritual energy that I guide through my will and bestow upon you.

LETTER EIGHTEEN

WHAT GOD IS

PEOPLE WHO ARE AT HOME IN THEIR PARticular field of expertise and familiar with every aspect and detail of it often assume that others are equally conversant with the knowledge in their field. It can come as a surprise to them to realize that concepts and language they take for granted may be completely foreign or at least new to others. I find myself in a similar position when I am called to describe in words matters concerning the eternal Spirit. Despite the fact that I carefully evaluate the effect of the words I choose from all angles, in the end I must often face the fact that an expression I have used may be misinterpreted, or that words that I use as synonyms seem to readers to refer instead to different things. Because I am conscious of the structure of life within the eternal Spirit through my own experience of the eternal realm, the meaning of my words may seem apparent to me—and therefore safe from misinterpretation—until a question is put to me that forces me to discover, to my dismay, that I have been misunderstood.

The question you posed concerning the concept "God" in your recent letter, however, is an example of a different sort of misunderstanding. Whereas readers usually think words that I use as synonyms refer to different things, I see that you, on the other hand, are thinking the opposite: that words I am using to differentiate between concepts are synonymous. But you are mistaken—even though I can understand why you would come to this conclusion.

We are dealing here with realities within the structure of spiritual life that cannot be fathomed by the intellect and are virtually impossible to express in words without the risk of misunderstanding. This risk is exacerbated by the fact that, when I speak of God, most people immediately assume I am referring to the conventional concept of God that is embedded in their consciousness. I use the term "God" in quite a different sense, not as a postulate of faith but as the consciousness of self that exists within the innermost of all eternal spiritual Reality. This is the only meaning that I wish my readers to give to the word "God." This innermost consciousness of the Eternal is not of a fixed or intellectual nature but, rather, generates itself ever anew out of the inexhaustible sea of that same eternal Spirit—it is the essence of the eternal, living Spirit that flows out of the infinite universe and is the only thing that *is*, infusing all with its sublime light. At the same time it is eternal Will—ever-active and inexhaustible energy manifesting in varying degrees of intensity and mildness according to its own inherent laws.

Do not search for God in the abyss
the menacing depths or frightening cliffs
Do not search for God in roaring waters
in surging oceans where storm winds blow
Do not search for God where lightning flashes
  and thunder shakes the earth
Do not search for God in distant worlds
  and far-off suns
nor in the intoxication of sensual delights

If you would find God within your self
you must overcome fear and grasping
Do not dream of distances beyond your reach
God is closer to you than the stars

All things are in God, and God is in all things. God emanates from three spheres of origin: Primordial Being, Primordial Light, and Primordial Word, and in its manifestation as the Father.* God is in all visible and invisible life.

One should not take these words to mean that I am preaching some kind of pantheism, nor is it my intention to imply that God is like a person. Primordial Being, Primordial Light and Primordial Word are not "persons" and do not equate to the Christian doctrine of the Trinity: Father, Son and the Holy Ghost. Similarly, that which the Luminaries of Primordial Light mean by "the Father" is entirely different from the meaning that concept has in Christian doctrine.

We know and teach Reality, not religious doctrine.

In the realm of Reality—that is, in the structure of life within the eternal Spirit—monotheistic

---

* In his other writings, Bô Yin Râ makes it clear that one could just as well refer to God as "the Mother." For example, in *The Path of My Pupils* he writes: "I endeavor to show how this Primordial Human of the Spirit is both Father and Mother to the human being..." (The Kober Press, 2017, p.110).

and polytheistic explanations for what God is can coexist without in any way contradicting one another.

People commonly refer to God as "the highest being" but the God of Reality is not that. Rather, the concept of "the highest being" is best expressed as God's manifestation as the Father who, in turn, radiates himself in the form of the twelve Fathers, each of which represents an aspect of his being. God, however, is not a "being" but, rather, a *beingness* that penetrates and imbues everything that is intrinsically *real*—that is, everything that exists in the realm of Eternity. The word "beingness" is to be understood here in a special, singular sense. That which is true of God is also true of Primordial Being, Primordial Light, and Primordial Word, and also of the Father in all his aspects.

The Father, however, is the *aspect of humanness* within Primordial Being, Primordial Light, and Primordial Word: the Primordial Human Being of the Spirit who is forever begetting itself. The Father is the ordering principle in all things that emanate from him and, therefore, also the ordering principle of that which is eternal in mortal human beings.

God is just as fully God within the Twelve Fathers—the form in which the Father is revealed—as within Primordial Being, Primordial Light, and Primordial Word. That which is "God" is only "God" for and within itself—beingness for and within itself. However, from the perspective of all those who are unified with God within the eternal, radiant Spirit's life, God is the *beingness* of all beings. And beings are *real* to the extent to which they embody the quality of beingness.

I am not juxtaposing ideas here or superimposing one concept upon another; rather, I am describing the interpenetrating nature of the structure of eternal spiritual Life, as far as the words of human language allow.

One should not suppose that a description of eternal Reality is of little use to humans, given that they need to search for solutions to the completely different and more immediate, pressing problems of physical existence. Be that as it may, no human beings on earth can find the inner peace and the salvation of the soul that they consciously or unconsciously long for if their conceptual world is not aligned with the way in which eternal life in the realm of the Spirit is ordered.

As you can see, your question was not at all in danger of being considered "inappropriate or superfluous" by me, as you thought it might be. Even the slightest deviation from Reality in your understanding of the structure of eternal, spiritual life can block you from reaching your goal—that is, from honing your ability to perceive and assimilate that which is of the Spirit.

May you always be open to receiving the blessings of the Light.

LETTER NINETEEN

BEING AND BEINGNESS

YOU ARE MISTAKEN IF YOU BELIEVE THAT I might become impatient because you are once again needing to ask me a question. In fact, I can well understand the source of your confusion: You are puzzled to see the words "being" (*Wesen*) and "beingness" (*Wesenheit*), which I have used synonymously in other of my writings, to signify different things here.

My intention, of course, is to present whatever I wish to communicate as clearly as possible. In this case, however, I see no other linguistic possibility but to ask the reader to accept the term "beingness" (*Wesenheit*) to mean that which confers "being" (*Wesen*). Thus, the Highest Being (*das höchste Wesen*) is a being (*Wesen*) because it is within beingness (*Wesenheit*) and because beingness

(*Wesenheit*) is within it. I simply must have both words (*Wesen* and *Wesenheit*) at my disposal if I am to communicate what I wish my readers to understand. It is like trying to explain to someone who has risen from the dead after one hundred years that an electric motor only moves if it is powered—that is, moved—by electricity. Here I would need to use both the words "moved," for that which is moved, and "moves," for that which creates the movement. I must admit, however, that this comparison is flawed because to me "beingness" is not only that which animates a being, but primarily a being's innermost self—its living core.

I am far from playing a game with words here, nor do I wish to argue about the conventional meanings that are assigned to the words in question. I give you full permission to replace the word "beingness"—through which "being" is made possible—with any other word you find more suitable.

My sole concern is that you understand my *meaning*. I ask you to try to *feel* your way into the meaning—to feel it as I feel it. What I am trying to describe is completely removed from the realm of thought and can never be expressed by even the most precise descriptions.

There is no easy way to insure that you do not misinterpret what I have written about the birth of the Living God in your eternal soul. Thus, I cannot spare you the effort necessary to feel your way into the meaning I am trying to convey. We are dealing here with "beingness"—that through which "being" is made possible—and it is the experience of beingness which is the birth of the Living God within. Each individual can become conscious of the Living God within, which is beingness, and each will experience it differently, in a manner that corresponds to his or her individual nature. It is only through this inner birth that human beings can attain beingness in the realm of time and in Eternity.

The Father is only accessible to the Luminaries of Primordial Light—who are his procreation—in his manifestation as the Twelve Fathers. Each individual Luminary is conscious of the Father only in the form of that unique father among the Twelve Fathers —all of whom are *identical* with the Father— who begot this particular Luminary within the Primordial Word. The Living God of whom

I speak, however, is the only self-revelation of God that can be reached by every human being on earth insofar as they have been able to prepare themselves for this experience within the soul. I use the analogy to a birth to describe the "birth" of the Living God within the soul.

Finally, keep in mind that my sole purpose in writing my books has been to guide seekers onto the right path so that they may prepare themselves to reach the inner goal. Almost all human beings today, with the exception of a vanishing few, are so deeply immersed in their thoughts—in a consciousness centered solely in mental activity—that they take their thoughts to be Reality. Even the dullest among them, who are satisfied with limited, simple thoughts, feel that they are living real life when they live only in their thoughts.

Given all this, in order to provide the right guidance I needed to make clear what place the experience of one's Living God has within the overall structure of eternal, spiritual life. There was no other way to accomplish this except by describing all those facets encompassed by eternal life in the radiant Spirit that might in some way help to clarify things.

I could not leave out anything that might help merely because that particular aspect could not be experienced by everyone. I had to include a great deal so that some of my readers would choose to pursue at least a little; that is, the minimum of what is required of them in order to succeed on their quest.

May you feel within yourself the blessings I send you. May you come to understand with ever greater clarity that every description of matters having to do with life within the realm of Spirit is hampered by the impossibility of putting this Reality into words.

LETTER TWENTY

QUESTIONS I DO NOT WANT TO BE ASKED

YOU WILL ALWAYS FIND ME READY TO help seekers on the path to becoming conscious of the eternal Spirit. I will gladly make every effort to help you and other seekers successfully complete the preparations that must be completed if you are to experience the birth of the Living God within your souls. But I must ask you to never pressure me to discuss matters concerning earthly problems—an area I must categorically avoid if I am to do justice to the spiritual tasks that only I am able to perform.

I must protect the cell in which I live
from the noise of the world
the trivia and fuss
over things that change
with the winds.

I cannot discourse with the many
and at the same time act within the Spirit
to loosen the bonds which bind humanity
the bonds which must be loosened
if mortals are to find the Light.

It is not indifference to the commonplace troubles of my fellow human beings that leads me to firmly turn away all questions that do not deal with the realm of the eternal Spirit. There are enough people who dedicate themselves to solving such problems. However, at the present time and until the very distant future there is not a single human being aside from myself who can carry out the purely spiritual task of transmitting the help that the Spirit offers to all those able to receive its blessings—while *at the same time* communicating, through the medium of a single language, the authentic nature and reality of the Spirit. I must conserve my energies and expend them only to help my fellow mortals through the unique work that has been made possible for me alone. Others who attempt this work will do so in vain; they would be trying to master a task through their earthly being that I am able to fulfill only because I can do so using my *eternal* being.

I do not wish to use words that over the course of two thousand years have been revered as sacred by those who venerate the one who first uttered them.* I must, nevertheless, speak of the eternal realm of the Spirit from whence I originate. There I live in indissoluble union with the Father through the particular one of the Twelve Fathers whose nature is best suited to my own and through whom the Father spiritually begat me in the primordial Light. My earthly self has come into existence through the soul who offered its physical body to me within the realm of the Spirit, long before the earth was created. My earthly being derives its meaning and exists solely to fulfill the pledge it made eons ago to serve me, the being begotten of the Spirit in this, the time on earth destined for me. Thus, I seek to make use of it to give expression *only to matters of the Father.* It would be truly remarkable if my earthly being could also serve other things.

In my books I show how all matters between birth and death can be shaped and lived in such a way that their effects on the invisible

---

* This is a reference to Jesus of Nazareth.

realm, all the way into the worlds of eternal Spirit, can powerfully help the soul to advance.

Those seeking guidance on how to live should look at the passages in my books that deal with these matters. There they will find the sought-for advice readily at hand and need only adapt what I have written to their particular cases. To be sure, individuals will also have to look beyond the temporal details of their situations in order to fully discern the deeper meaning of my words.

Because of my special situation, I must ask you to consult what I have written and find your own answers rather than ask me. Were I to get involved in the ever-changing earthly problems and questions of individuals—which are, after all, their own affair and responsibility—I would be transgressing the requirements of the structure of eternal, spiritual life in which my being is embedded and from which my work must proceed.

I am sure you can understand that, if no such obligation stood in my way, it would be easy for me to formulate answers to your questions. But then you would be compelled to agree with my answers, even if they were far removed from your own thoughts about the matter. It is just this kind of undue influence which, though unintended, is inevitable, and that the law of the Spirit, which I am obligated to obey, prohibits.

May you find what is fitting for you *within yourself*, guided by the blessings of the Light.

LETTER TWENTY-ONE

THE NUMBER TWELVE AND THE BELL TOWER CLOCK

If you wish to regard the Father—who is not accessible to your consciousness although your life emanates from His being—as a unity that experiences itself in the form of twelve reflections of its being, you certainly are not straying from reality. But you must also add a thirteenth aspect that describes the all-encompassing unity that is formed by these twelve reflections—just as the wisdom-filled initiates of olden times used to do. This is the same reality that is being referred to when the Gospels speak of Jesus having had twelve disciples, with Jesus being the thirteenth who spiritually encompassed them all.

I leave it to archeologists to decide whether the twelve Gods of the Egyptians, the Greeks, the earliest inhabitants of Italy, and the Romans who came after them also refer to this spiritual reality of the Father. That there were female figures to be found among these twelve gods is irrelevant to the question.

Although I am grateful to the science of archeology for a number of accounts that relate to my own spiritual experience, I do not know whether there are any archeological findings that point to the existence of a deity who is either a part of or encompasses these twelve aspects of god. The existence of the thirteenth being, however, is central if one is to understand that the worship of the twelve gods is directly connected to the worship of the eternal Father. As for the circle of twelve around Jesus, one could have easily named less than or more than twelve disciples if it were not the intent of the author to draw a parallel with the Father-mystery. I do not mean to cast doubt on the historical authenticity of each of those twelve named when I say that this circle and Jesus together symbolize the spiritual reality of the Father. My point here is that in Jesus's time this mystery was known not only to select initiates but to entire mystery cults, and it is from these mystery cults that many of the followers of Jesus's teachings later emerged.

However, your question as to the nature of the Father indicates to me a certain readiness to engage in useless cogitation that will not further you on your path one whit.

As important as it may be for you to attain a clear concept of God, it is not necessary to belabor all new insights gained on your path by trying to analyze all possible interpretations. If the clock in the bell tower strikes seven you need only hear the number of strikes in order to know the hour. It doesn't matter if you also realize that that, although the strokes of the clock may occur at even intervals, the tone of the bells may impart a certain rhythm to the whole. Thus the bells could sound like this:

1 2 **3** 4 **5** 6 **7**

or like this:

1 2 **3** 4 5 6 **7**

or also like this:

1 2 3 **4** 5 6 **7**

If the thought suddenly occurs to you that a spiritual truth you heard from me could also be expressed differently, then feel free to follow your thought. But take your realization in stride and do not allow yourself to become excited—to imagine that you are an explorer discovering new lands. Too much excitement would disturb and spoil the calm perspective from which you have learned to view and understand what has already become clear to you. There can be many ways of viewing, many ways of conceiving of a thing, and all can be correct as long as they result in a clear, undistorted picture of that which needs to be understood.

It is the *result* that justifies your efforts at understanding. It matters not whether you unlock the cabinet door by holding the key in the lock while two helpers turn the cabinet around the key's axis or whether you select the slightly simpler method of inserting the key into the lock and turning it, while leaving the cabinet where it is.

In the same way, if you feel the need to use your mental faculties in order to comprehend something within the soul, you should focus your thoughts on the goal and the best way to achieve it, and not allow yourself to become diverted. However, you should also not declare war on all other thoughts under the fond illusion that you will then be able to commune undisturbed with a desired thought on an empty battlefield. In order for your mental efforts to be effective—something often necessary in daily life as well—consider the following analogy: When looking for a particular object on the horizon from a distant vantage point, the searcher's glance will land on many forms. In the attempt to locate that one particular form, these other forms do not disappear, nor are they perceived as an interference by the person searching; the searcher is too intently focused on being able to distinguish a close-up, distinct image of the form being sought. But it is precisely this focus on a close-up image which prevents that person from finding the sought–after form. Once the searcher realizes that only a distant image, appearing alongside many other forms, is all that can be expected, the sought–after form is soon found. For instance, if the sought-for, close-up image is a mighty tower, perhaps only a silhouette the size of a needlepoint jutting out from the haze, among all the other forms, can be seen. However, the searcher now knows how to hold fast to this remote image or how to easily locate it again without feeling disturbed by all the other forms on the horizon.

It is easy to see how this analogy can be applied to situations in the invisible realm of thought. If your goal is to be able to concentrate fully on a particular subject or theme, you must have a realistic idea of how it will reveal itself and how it can be recognized when seen from the "vantage point" you have achieved in your inner development. In the realm of thought there are laws of "perspective" akin to the laws that govern perspective in the visual world.

Once you have a clear sense of the form in which the sought-for subject or theme will be found, it should be looked for in this way and, having found it, focused on in your thoughts. All other thoughts that may enter your consciousness are to be ignored—but not fought. If you fight unwanted thoughts you will give them energy and activate them and it will become impossible to ignore them. The searchers who have found the church spire they have been seeking will see everything in their field of vision—but all these other things will hardly enter their awareness as long as they are inwardly occupied with the sought-for image.

May this letter, as with my previous letters, help you with any difficulties you have encountered.

May you receive every blessing!

LETTER TWENTY-TWO

THE BLINDERS THAT MUST FALL FROM ONE'S EYES

I AM VERY HAPPY TO HEAR THAT CERTAIN things have become clear to you and that you feel as if your eyes have finally been opened, now that you have made certain discoveries about the meaning of my words. I still regard as valid the reasons that led me to be less than explicit in some of what I describe in *The Book on the Living God*—to cloak the meaning, as it were, under a protective veil. Even so, my heart was heavy when I finally allowed the book to be published. I can understand how liberating it must have felt to you to finally know with certainty what lies hidden from unwelcome glances.

It was also my intention, by expressing certain things in a veiled manner, to give my readers the freedom to conceive of the spiritual community of the Luminaries of Eternal Light in their own way. I did not want them to feel *compelled* to accept an article of faith—and to then shy away from it as a result. Now that you have recognized that the "head" of the Luminaries is indeed the Father, you can see that the truth was in no way harmed by being presented in an obscured manner. Although he is neither "elected" nor "nominated," no doubt ever exists among the Luminaries as to who this head truly is. We, the Luminaries of Eternal Light, are his spiritually begotten sons, each serving at his preordained place within the structure of spiritual Life.

I certainly did not doubt that the images and parables I make use of might be misunderstood, but I never thought that those readers for whom my books were actually written would misunderstand me—if I had not experienced it so often. Even you say that only now have the blinders "finally fallen from your eyes."

It appears, however, that such blinders still cover many eyes that I had believed to be wide open and not in need of liberation. Is it really so difficult to comprehend the deeper meaning of that which I so carefully veiled in order to protect it from the impure glances of those for whom it was not intended?

As for myself, I often feel relieved and even joyful when I am misunderstood because it would be disturbing to be understood by *everyone*. I reveal myself *solely* for those who are *capable of awakening* in the Spirit—and the obligation to reveal myself is a burden truly not to be desired.

There are numerous passages, especially in my first books, where I had just barely overcome the resistance of my mortal self and felt myself able to publically acknowledge my eternal spiritual nature—only to try to immediately hide again behind my earthly identity. This option to disappear behind my mortal self in my writings was made possible by the fortunate fact that I could use the pronoun "I" to refer to either my transient, mortal self or to my eternal, spiritual being.

In telling you this, I am not disclosing a secret. I have just recently published three little books of poetry in which, in rhythmic form, I reveal things about my nature that a mortal human can only bring himself to reveal with great difficulty and then only when not doing so would have consequences of life and death importance. In the case of these books of poetry I felt there were reasons substantial enough for me to make them public.

But even those who make disclosures to the public about their eternal nature with some frequency find satisfaction in reflecting upon their eternal self, whose consciousness is anchored in Eternity, from the perspective of their transient, mortal nature. Thus, it is left to you to intuit what is truly being said in any given passage, keeping in mind that I did not want to suppress the expression of my mortal being—which makes it possible for me to reveal myself to other mortals—for the sake of expressing my eternal being more directly.

The perception of the eternal realm varies in important ways depending on how particular human mortals arrive at that perception: that is, whether individuals gain insight into matters of the Spirit through meditation and the struggles of the soul, or whether they experience their eternal self through the eternal being with whom they are united, in spirit and in body, and who they are here on earth to serve for the benefit of all humanity.

From the time I first began to publish my books, I was well aware that I was expecting a lot from my readers—and that it is exceedingly rare to find individuals who have the ability to perceive what I convey in my writings and do what is required for their soul's awakening.

In my books, I speak of a bearer of eternal consciousness who unites with both the physical body and eternal soul of a human of this earth—thus fusing all into one. I also describe that this union takes place because of a voluntary commitment made by this human's eternal, spiritual self, eons ago, before he became incarnated on earth. Modern Europeans will no doubt think of all this as an absurd fantasy that can only be excused as possibly resulting from mental illness. One must not blame them for the absolute ignorance of their souls in the face of timeless Reality. They cannot help it!

It is not surprising then, that I am all the more pleased when I encounter unexpected exceptions to this impediment to understanding. Your kind and detailed letter shows me that you are one of these welcome exceptions; your words have brought me joy and will continue to do so.

If you can resolve to read all my books again—now that you have sought to both understand them intellectually and to make them a possession of your soul—it will seem to you as if you had never read them at all. This is how different your understanding will be of many passages that had previously been unclear to you.

May all the blessings from the eternal, spiritual Light in which I dwell be with you.

LETTER TWENTY-THREE

NO TWO INDIVIDUALS ARE THE SAME BEFORE GOD

YOU ARE QUITE RIGHT TO POINT OUT that the boundary between what is possible for every individual to experience in the eternal Spirit and that which only a Luminary of Primordial Light may experience is not always clearly delineated in my writings. What you could not possibly know, however, is that this apparent flaw is determined and demanded by the nature of eternal Reality.

Consider that within all earthly human beings, along with the physical body and the animal soul that comes into being with the birth of the physical body and will dissolve again at its death, there also dwells an *eternal* self—although for many people the eternal self may remain in a latent state during their lifetime. This eternal scintilla, this everlasting spark of the Spirit, expresses and experiences itself through the eternal soul that surrounds it and that forms itself out of the eternal soul forces. It fulfills a uniquely determined role—the role reserved for *it alone*—within the structure of eternal life in the realm of the Spirit, just as the Luminary of Primordial Light takes his own place therein. The Luminary who fulfills his tasks while incarnated in an earthly body has been *unified* with a particular mortal's scintilla of the Spirit eons ago and, with it, this scintilla's eternal soul forces so that, in the end, this mortal's physical body and animal soul come under the influence of the eternal Luminary whose instruments they are, as long as the mortal being remains on earth.

The Luminary of Primordial Light is endowed with the ability to experience everything that is possible within the life of the eternal Spirit, right to the innermost core of this life, because his consciousness flows from out of this realm. However, he can only share this way of experiencing with that individual, eternal human spirit who had already united with him in the Spirit's realm so that, through this human, the Luminary might provide spiritual help to all on earth. This task can be accomplished only because, millennia before the particular human spirit is destined to become incarnated in a physical body, the Luminary takes this human spirit into his own self and fuses with him, thus allowing this human spirit to partake of the Luminary's experience of life within the Spirit. This "being taken into the self" of the Luminary is the consequence, determined by spiritual law, of the commitment, freely-made by the human spirit an unimaginable time ago, so that this human is now privileged to undergo a mystery-filled preparation. With regard to all other eternal, spiritual scintillas incarnated in the earthly realm, the Luminaries of Primordial Light can only help them to become aware of and master their eternal soul forces so that they may come to know themselves through the consciousness inherent in their soul, and be able to shape and unite with the form of soul that suits their individual spiritual natures.

There is a constant interplay between the eternal soul forces and brain-based modes of perception, feeling, and experience. Because of this, the mental concepts of human beings can play a decisive role in furthering the awakening of their souls. Conversely, the eternal Spirit, through the pathway of the individualized form of the Spirit—the eternal, spiritual scintilla of the individual human being—can gradually penetrate the physical body such that this body is able to become the embodiment of the Spirit on earth.

Every human being's spiritual self is unique and, therefore, corresponds only with a very specific form of spiritual experience, accessible only to that person. Because the variations in these forms of spiritual experience are infinite in number, it is impossible to describe them all or even to characterize them by group. However, because the proper development of our conceptual world is of immeasurable importance for our spiritual unfolding, it is advisable for seekers to have a good idea of the kind of spiritual experience they may expect. They should be aware of all the different kinds of experience possible, and this is why I have been specific in my descriptions, rather than simply making general remarks. As I told you some time ago, seekers who are honest with themselves will intuitively know which of my writings are meant for them. However, they will gain a greater and deeper insight into the nature of all things spiritual if they also find out about other possibilities, even as they intuitively sense that these paths are not meant for them, though they may lead others to the goal.

Although every spiritual self is unique, people persist in believing that all humans are the same before God—an idea that refuses to die and yet is contrary to spiritual Reality. It is the product of dark and barren atavistic beliefs that arise from the animal origins of our physical bodies, which are formed from the matter of this planet. Only a god lacking in originality would create a world in which all humans come into it with the same spiritual core. It is a comfort to then consider that this unimaginative god is the product of nothing better than these outmoded ways of thinking. From the vantage point of spiritual Reality, there is *infinite variety* in the relationships to God within the structure of life in the realm of the eternal Spirit. The idea of sameness before God is only accurate when one is referring to the physical, animal nature of the human being that arises from this planet and, in its given time, must return to it. But when one considers the spiritual aspect—the individual spiritual scintillas—of the dual-natured creatures on earth who like to think that they embody the essence of what it means to be human, we see that they differ more from each other than any group of forms on earth. These great differences exist not only in the form of each human scintilla but also in how each human spirit fits into its sharply defined, hierarchical place within the world of Spirit.

Nothing can be altered here by applying philosophical concepts that are so foreign to the realm of Reality that they have no presence at all in this realm—not even as faint shadows.

Nor can anything be acquired here, because everything another person has in the realm of Spirit is their inalienable possession, just as one's own spiritual possessions belong to each of us alone.

As you can see, sharp distinctions exist with regard to the range of experiences possible among individual spiritual entities, such that the surface of the earth would not suffice to hold all those differences. By contrast, it is impossible to make a similar sharp division between what only a Luminary of Primordial Light may experience and that which every human spirit may experience after the awakening of their soul—the sharper division that you were hoping I would able to point out to you—because they constitute two very distinct kinds of experience. The experience of a Luminary encompasses *infinity* whereas that of most human beings is limited by their ability to experience spiritual life.

May you dwell within the blessing of the Light.

LETTER TWENTY-FOUR

ON PROFESSING BEFORE OTHERS

THE QUESTION YOU ASK IN YOUR LATEST letter to me is one that I was certain I would hear from you eventually and I am only surprised you did not ask it sooner. I am also amazed that so few seekers have asked me this question. It is as if they are afraid my answer might be one they would rather not hear.

Christian believers all know that Jesus is supposed to have said: "But whosoever shall deny me before men, him will I also deny before my Father which is in heaven." (Matthew 10:33 KJV) You are wondering how to reconcile the threatening tone of these words with my admonition to not proselytize and are concerned that you will be barred from making progress on the spiritual path if you do not profess to others that you are a reader of my books.

To be sure, Jesus did not intend these words as a threat. But the threatening tone of the version that has come down to us suited the purposes of the growing Christian cult that followed his death, which was competing for adherents with the other mystery cults of the time—all of whom were struggling to distinguish themselves from the Judaism of the ancient world, which bound the Jewish people together. It is ironic that Jesus, who was himself a Jew, was the inspiration for these cults—although that certainly was not his intention. Borrowing concepts from other mystery cults of the time, the early Christians considered Jesus to be the anointed one to be worshipped as the central figure of their mystery cult. As such, they decided that he *must* have spoken in this or that way—and therefore determined that he *had* actually spoken in this way.

At this time the reports of his life and teachings were simply read aloud as part of the cult's ceremonial worship and were not yet considered to be "Holy Scripture." Nevertheless there was a rationale for the threatening slant given to Jesus's words. Jesus had indeed once pointed out that "no man can serve two masters" (Matthew 6:24 KJV), that is to say, if one lives one's outer life in a way contrary to what the insights of one's soul require, one betrays oneself. A person's actions on earth must be in alignment with *eternal* laws: Human beings cannot live their outer lives according to one set of standards while at the same time fooling themselves into believing they are adhering to another to achieve their eternal salvation. It was easy to twist the true meaning of Jesus's words and use them to make the listening public fearful for their souls—a fear that has to do with the soul of the human *animal* and not the eternal soul. In this way the new mystery cult was able to take advantage of people's psychological vulnerabilities and manipulate them into joining the cult.

People spoke in absolute terms in those days; no room was left for questioning or doubt. And no one can doubt that the leaders of the new mystery cult had a correct understanding of the psychological makeup of their fellow humans. The Master of Nazareth, the Kyrios, the Anointed One, from now on was held to have said that he would not acknowledge before the Heavenly Father those members of the new mystery cult formed around his name who were not ready to testify before others that he was the ultimate fulfillment of the yearnings of their soul during their life on earth.

However, one ought also not doubt that a spiritual practice that is sporadic and less than fully committed—and a commitment to spiritual practice is at the core of the teachings of Jesus—is frivolous play and is not recognized in the realm of the Spirit. In fact, such irreverent behavior may be counterproductive in that it may trigger defensive energies in the Spirit that will bar seekers from further progress—energies which have shocked and disquieted the souls of those on earth who have witnessed the effects of their implacable justice. Thus, in a certain sense, the threatening tone inserted into the words of Jesus after his death can indeed be understood to express an unyielding truth: that adherence to spiritual teaching does not lead to the desired goal if one does not use it to guide one's conduct in the outside world.

You now find yourself faced with the obligation to apply my teachings to your behavior in the world around you. You say that you are prepared to do this but are not quite sure how to proceed. This question is entirely different from your desire to understand how to behave with regard to being a reader of my books and acknowledging their influence upon you.

In *The Path of My Pupils* I explain how mistaken it is to try and convert others to my teachings. I hardly need to warn you about this sort of misstep. In addition, one fails to understand why my books exist and that they are unique and anchored in the eternal realm if one believes—filled with the best intentions to propagate these books—that one should try to create some sort of official religious body to promote them in the outside world.

Despite what I had to say in *The Path of My Pupils*, I do not wish to give the impression that I consider it undesirable to recommend one of my books the way one would, for example, recommend a particularly well-written novel. I merely caution against intrusive "missionary zeal" and against appointing one's self as an apostle, in the mistaken assumption that my books need apostles. On the other hand you should feel free, when you think it appropriate, to tell others that you follow my teachings and to refer to me by name. Needless to say, this should be done in a dignified manner—just as scholars might name the founder of a school of thought to which they adhere along with colleagues who are similarly influenced by that school of thought.

It is also generally understood and a matter of common literary etiquette that one should clearly name the source if one quotes from my books or feels one's self inspired by my words. After all, the things I disclose have been cast into form by me and this form is my intellectual property. I do not wish my writings to be plundered under the pretext that we are dealing with teachings bestowed by the Spirit. Not only is the artistic form my exclusive property but also the style and order in which I present my teachings.

In your letter you ask how your progress on the spiritual path should influence your behavior in the outside world. And here it will not be difficult to understand that all things must gradually disappear from your life that cannot be brought into complete harmony with the teachings given in my books. It should be equally easy to understand that it is not enough to merely avoid what cannot be brought into such harmony: You have a moral duty to more and more consciously and intentionally shape your life and align everything you do or say to reflect what is positive in my advice. When I refer to your speech, I do not mean that you should parrot my words. Rather, when you reflect within yourself, your speech should be congruent with my teachings.

The more you try to put into practice the insights gained from my books of spiritual guidance, the more you will also serve the world around you.

Having said this, I shall now end my letter and hope that I have answered all aspects of your question. May you be blessed in all the good that you bring to the outside world, in accordance with the laws of Spirit.

LETTER TWENTY-FIVE

MASTERS WHO HAVE FALLEN

YOU HAVE ASKED ME ABOUT THOSE PASsages in my books where I discuss the eventuality that a Luminary of Primordial Light who has been incarnated so as to serve as a spiritual helper on earth may nonetheless fall from grace through his own terrible doing. Indeed, there have been such cases of masters who have fallen as a result of their own sacrilege since ancient times. You wanted to know if you have correctly understood what I have said about these unfortunate souls and I can confirm that you have.

Practically speaking, however, the accuracy of your understanding has little relevance to your inner growth. In order to find your own path into the spirit it is not necessary to have a detailed understanding of the passages in question. On the other hand, it is certainly best not to tolerate even the slightest ambiguity in one's thoughts, which is why I welcome your determined pursuit for clarity concerning the most terrible thing that can happen here on earth.

When I wrote the passages in question I certainly did not think any reader would lose sleep over them. Otherwise, I would have added further clarification as a matter of course so as to not leave any gaps in the narrative. But why would I have considered further clarification to be necessary? I could not imagine that my discerning readers would come to the conclusion that a Luminary of Primordial Light—an eternal being spiritually begotten of the Father and sent into this earthly realm to be of service to humanity—could, under any circumstances, experience his gradual spiritual dissolution into a harrowing night lasting eons. Nor could I have supposed, after everything I have written elsewhere about the eternal scintilla dwelling in every mortal human being that, in the end, my readers would think this eternal spiritual pole could be subject to dissolution. I have also clearly written that when the *soul* has become a kingdom of Eternity and its bearer has been accepted into the circle of Luminaries, its crown and scepter can never be lost except through the actions of the human being who carries the Luminary with whom he is united. Aside from your last letter, though, I have never received any correspondence suggesting that my words on this subject have caused a reader difficulties. And it appears that you have succeeded in finding the right answers to your own questions concerning the relevant passages.

The Luminary of Primordial Light who enters the earthly realm unites so completely with that particular, eternal human spirit who freely pledged himself to this union inconceivably long ago while in the spiritual realm, and with the physical being that carries this eternal human spirit on earth, such that one must rightly speak of their complete fusion during their earthly sojourn. As a result of this fusion a soul is formed that can sense and take part in the consciousness of every aspect of this fused entity. This soul is not lost to the eternal human spirit and to the eternal Luminary after their incarnation on earth has ended—unless condemned to dissolution by the misconduct of the mortal human in which it dwells. But even there when its dissolution becomes inevitable through the hubris of the mortal creature that is part of the fused entity, the primal *energies* that formed the fused soul are *not* lost. These sublime energies, or soul forces, form the communal soul shared by a Luminary and the human spirit connected with him; but now, after dissolving out of the once integrated, communal soul, they revert back into the form from which they originally emanated. This can be described as a dissolution of consciousness of the soul through loss of the eternal "I," while the eternal "I" itself remains inviolable within the realm of Spirit, as does the Luminary to whom it had once pledged itself.

The only way the mortal mind can grasp what I have tried to indicate here—as you have—is by conceiving of it in the following way: Nothing that is eternal can be destroyed. Therefore, we must be dealing with a form of mortal consciousness that was intended to serve the Eternal but had the hubris to imagine itself too important to remain devoted to that aspect of its entity that exists solely in the realm of the Spirit.

Such a loss of the soul occurs daily on a smaller scale among human beings on earth who, to be sure, are not united with a Luminary. I have written enough about this in my books. After their physical death, those who have become soulless are forced—just as is the case with a fallen Luminary—to experience harrowing darkness and the agonizing, gradual dissolution of consciousness, condemned for eons to know that this agony will continue, without being able to prevent it. Yet all these instances of soul disintegration do not in any way affect the *eternal* nature of the soul forces that had come together to form these souls, now lost and condemned to gradual dissolution. The cause of such self-imposed soul murder is always and in every case an individual's arrogant turning away from the Light that is consciousness of the Eternal.

To value one's eternal self above all
and live always in the light of the eternal
presence
truly is more difficult
than any pursuit on earth.
How hard it is for time-bound mortals
to forgo their earthly strivings
a sacrifice too great for most to bear.

The never-ending tragedy of human beings is that they cause their own downfall by pursuing the very things they believe will save them—by valuing those earthly strivings that raise them above bare existence and imagining that those alone will sustain them.

May this reply to your most welcome letter also answer questions that you have not yet even asked.

May you always remain within the blessing of the Light!

LETTER TWENTY-SIX

RADIANT STONES AND SUBSTANCES

DON'T WORRY ABOUT WEARING THE artistically crafted ring you have inherited—a valuable family heirloom—even if a friend who swears by astrology has frightened you with his foolish warning that aquamarine is "not your stone." The positive feelings that you have for this stone are far surer proof that its vibrations are in harmony with your nature than any advice of an astrologer. Astrologers cannot help but deliver flawed results even if they are correct on certain points. Too much ancient astrological knowledge has been lost, misinterpreted, or even made up. Until a new, reliable body of empirical knowledge can be established the value of astrology will be limited to tentative insights about an individual's character—and then only when the time of birth of the subject in question can be accurately established. It goes without saying that the so-called horoscopes to be found in the advertising sections of newspapers should not be considered at all.

As far as matching certain gemstones with individual people is concerned, countless aspects of a person's horoscope must be taken into consideration. Most—if not all—of today's astrology experts and enthusiasts rely too much on the sign of the Zodiac under which the individual was born. Thus the horoscope may indicate that a certain stone is a match for a given individual, yet that person feels only an aversion for it. And this aversion is the best proof that the energies that radiate from these prescribed stones are in disharmony with the particular person's nature or, at best, do not resonate with the rhythm of that individual's life energies. The prescribed stones may actually be contra-indicated because they have an antagonistic effect on or work to diminish the person's life force. I have come across many such cases. When selecting gems, my advice has always been to be guided by one's feelings, as one's own feelings are more reliable for determining which stones are compatible than the best horoscope.

Bear in mind also that the effects of gemstones are limited to the wearer's physical, mortal body. Therefore, one should neither fear a negative influence on one's spiritual development nor expect a positive influence. At best one might say that gemstones have an *indirect* influence on one's spiritual progress. A particular gemstone may create a sense of harmony in the human beings who wear it so that, as a result, they may experience less interference from their animal nature as they strive to become conscious in the Spirit. In contrast, those who allow themselves to wear stones that do not resonate with or are antagonistic to their natures—perhaps because these gemstones are rare or expensive—are influenced, consciously or unconsciously, by the disharmony the stones create. This disharmony creates, in turn, a restlessness that works against the cultivation of the inner calm so necessary to all striving towards the Spirit.

In general, it should be noted that gemstones or even ordinary pebbles have a numerically-determined, cosmically-based relationship to the person who wears them. This relationship takes place in the earthly realm, through the radiation that emanates from the stones, and may have either a beneficial or a detrimental effect on the wearer. This effect may be almost imperceptible or extremely strong, depending upon the degree of affinity the individual has for the stone. Needless to say, this sort of affinity has nothing to do with a desire to possess a valuable object.

We are dealing here with something rather different from the animating force in amulets and talismans—unless these also contain gemstones, in which case a combination of energies may be at work. But where the radiation emanating from a stone is not involved, the power of the amulet or talisman derives solely from the *force of will* with which it has been imbued. The symbols and pictorial images visible on the object and their manifest or hidden meanings are not the source of its power. These symbols and pictorial images are valuable solely as points of focus for individuals intent on charging the amulets or talismans with the force of their will. It is only the *intensity of the charge* that is of importance. Thus even an otherwise insignificant object may serve as an amulet or talisman. For example, a small object that a mother, her heart aglow with love, presses into the hand of her son as he heads into danger, with the bid that he carry it always, can function as a talisman and afford him protection. You will find all this treated at length in the chapter "Faith, Talismans and Images of God" in *The Book on the Living God.*

As you can see, there is nothing uncanny at play here. One also does not need to immerse one's self in esoteric studies, like the few true adepts, if one wishes to make use of the planetary helping energies that radiate from stones, metals, colors, and forms to be found in nature, or to seek the protection true amulets and talismans can provide. Most importantly, you should never allow yourself to mistrust your own instincts, and be influenced instead by the advice of an "expert." Such interpretations, given the present state of knowledge, are always of questionable value. The more clearly you let your feelings "speak" without letting your thoughts intrude, the more you will be able to make the right choice and act correctly with regard to everything we have been speaking of.

May you also receive the blessings of eternal Light that will give you strength in spheres that planetary energies cannot reach.

The help that planetary energies
can give you here
extends no further than
your days on earth.
Once you have overcome
the deceptive light of earth's day
you will have found the Light
of the Eternal Day within yourself.

LETTER TWENTY-SEVEN

THE NEED TO DEVALUE SUFFERING

YOUR ROBUST PHYSICAL CONSTITUTION, which you say never really lets you experience physical pain, need not be an obstacle to understanding what I mean by the need to devalue suffering.* But keep in mind that I am not referring simply to *physical* pain when I speak of suffering. Emotional pain may befall persons who are virtually free from the ailments that can plague the physical body. And the most agonizing emotional suffering can be that which arises from witnessing and being concerned about the suffering of others.

When I speak of the need to devalue suffering, it matters not whether that suffering is physical or emotional—and the way to counter it is

---

* The need to devalue suffering is discussed in the book *Spirit and Form*, chapter five "Forming One's Grief."

the same. The most effective way to devalue suffering is to deprive it of the great pathos that has been accorded it through the centuries. Suffering has been endowed with a kind of reverence, instead of being regarded as something negative to be spurned and fought against. From a spiritual perspective, it is absolutely necessary to extinguish in oneself and others the foolish and even satanic notion that suffering is a divinely-ordained means for educating and punishing. This belief blocks people from realizing what an abhorrent concept of God is implied here. For those who are truly conscious of God, it is unbearably painful to see others endow God with such gruesome qualities and then hold out this image of God as a source of comfort to those who suffer. Even more appalling is the fact that sufferers will accept this God as a source of comfort. Here we see an extreme degree of passivity, an inability to offer resistance—and individuals who promote this sort of belief count on this passivity to get sufferers to acquiesce to it.

In stark contrast, anyone seeking to awaken in the realm of the eternal Spirit and to receive the Living God within themselves must avoid focusing on suffering and deny it any sort of moral significance. But do not misunderstand what I am saying here. When speaking of the need to devalue suffering I do not overlook the fact that emotional suffering may rouse those who merely "go through the motions" of life out of their torpor and inspire in them a new sense of purpose and that physical pain may play a necessary role in the process of healing. These are effects of which suffering may be the cause. From the spiritual perspective, however, suffering must always be understood to be a delusion. It seeks to beguile the human being's spiritual nature into believing it can be dominated and thus tries to bind it. But such subjugation only exists in this earthly realm and it is only the human being's animal nature that can be dominated—until that human being recognizes the delusion and thus deprives suffering of its power.

All suffering takes place solely in human beings' *animal nature,* which is their temporary form of manifestation here on earth. This animal nature has a soul that comes into existence as a function of the physical body and even the most gripping emotional suffering has reality only in this temporal, animal soul. To be sure, one should not imagine that the animal souls of earthly human beings are as limited in expression as the souls of other animals: The temporal soul is interconnected with the soul forces of the eternal soul—a soul possessed only by human beings and unaffected by the death of the body—and with the eternal soul's spiritual core. Because of this, the abilities of the human being's temporal, animal soul are greatly expanded. Thus the temporal soul receives such sublime influences from eternal, spiritual sources that almost everything that even those earthly human beings who know little about their true nature call the soul—those who believe in an eternal soul but have no experience of it or who imagine the soul to be something physical but far superior to other animals—is experienced within the highly developed *animal* soul of the mortal human being. This temporal soul is just as much a function of the human animal body as brain-based thought which, in the same way, far exceeds the thinking ability of animals.

As much as I value brain-based thinking—when applied to the spheres in which it is appropriate—I want to direct your attention to a different kind of thought: I am referring to the thought that thinks itself without use of the brain—although this thought makes itself known to human beings *through* the brain. While I admire what the animal soul that is part of the physical body of the human being has achieved, when I speak of the soul in my writings, I am referring almost always to the soul that is formed of *eternal* soul forces and, among all the animals on earth, is bestowed by the Spirit only upon human beings. The animal soul of the human being does not inspire in me the need to offer suggestions for its further development. Over the course of millennia the animal soul of humans has gradually reached such a state of development that, in most people, it almost completely smothers their eternal soul. It is high time for human beings to learn that a great part of what they consider to be their highest achievements is merely the product of the animal soul. This is true even when the temporal soul strives to deal as best it can with matters of Eternity—a realm that is in fact inaccessible to it. It is within this temporal soul that physical pain and everything referred to on earth as "emotional suffering" is experienced.

When I say that all suffering is a delusion, I certainly do not mean to deny that suffering can bring with it intense pain, which at times may seem unbearable. I myself am all too familiar with many forms of both physical and emotional suffering. What I do deny, however, is the over-emphasis on the significance of suffering and the reverential attitude with which human beings often regard it—as if suffering were a divinely ordained means for disciplining and teaching individuals.* By continuing to glorify suffering human beings merely create more suffering on this earth when they should, instead, make use of every possibility to avoid it.

The willingness of a Luminary of Primordial Light incarnated on earth to bear suffering is different from what is being discussed here. Rather, the Luminary's suffering is the price he *voluntarily* pays to the "Lord of Darkness" into whose realm he has penetrated—in violation

---

* "For whom the Lord loveth he chasteneth..." (Hebrews 12:6-7 KJV) Other translations of the Bible use the word "discipline" instead of "chasten." In Christian exegesis, this phrase is often interpreted to mean that God disciplines people in the same manner as a father might discipline his child.

of the laws of that realm. However, every kind of suffering, including the voluntary suffering of the Luminary, must be unmasked as an *evil* that takes place and is experienced within the animal nature. Because suffering is the inevitable result of physical laws, human beings have no choice but to bear it—but this has absolutely nothing to do with it being some kind of divinely ordained "education." When faced with emotional or physical suffering, humanity should call upon all its energies to ease and to end the pain.

Many religious faiths offer those who suffer "consolation" by convincing them that their pain is a form of divine discipline. But this belief has caused more preventable suffering among humans on earth than all the malice of human beings toward each other, through the inevitable chain of events in the invisible part of the physical world that such a belief sets into motion. This is where we see the "tormentors" of whom I spoke in *The Book on the Royal Art** at work.

* The reference is to page 101 of the original German-language edition, published in 1932; or page 82 of the English-language translation, published by The Kober Press in 2006.

These tormentors are living intelligences within the invisible, physical realm of the natural world. Suffering that is experienced in a visible, tangible physical body and its corresponding animal soul triggers in them an unrestrained lust. As a result, these vampire-like creatures use all of their considerable strength to cause, prolong and intensify the suffering of animals and humans—and even that which corresponds to suffering in the life of plants.

When suffering is accepted as being sent from God, the defensive powers of the human being's invisible physical dimension, that could otherwise offer resistance to the attempts of these tormentors to overwhelm the individual, are rendered powerless. Thus the unsuspecting victims themselves open the doors that bring more suffering into their lives. By contrast, animals are free to follow their instincts, and always try to evade suffering by resisting that which causes them discomfort.

The need to devalue suffering is of crucial importance and everyone should feel called to help with this effort once they have gained insight into what the transformation in their understanding of suffering means to themselves and to their fellow humans.

You too are called to help with this need.

May the Light of Eternity illuminate your way.

LETTER TWENTY-EIGHT

THE NATURE OF BLESSING AND HOW IT IS BESTOWED

IN OUR CORRESPONDENCE I HAVE OFTEN used the word *Segenswunsch* (blessing-wish) to convey my intention to send you blessings. Because I know what is truly meant by this word, I can assure you that you are correct in intuiting that a true blessing must be something "much more concrete" than just a well-meaning wish. Whenever I use the word *Segenswunsch*, I am referring to the *process* that must take place in order to bestow a true blessing on someone—and not simply to words that are conventionally used to convey a wish to send someone blessings.

Those who are truly able to bestow blessings—as I am able to do from my innermost being while I am here on earth—cannot do other than use this ability. At the same time, they may choose to use conventional language as a means of concealing from the outer world the sublime state of inner solemnity out of which true blessing takes place. In our Western world, persons who receive such blessings are generally unaware of the true nature of the blessings they have received—that someone might be able to bless them with a spiritual energy that is palpable—and so there is good reason for such concealment.

There are also other reasons which have led me to be careful about expressly stating that the act of blessing comes about through a transmission of eternal, spiritual Light that has actual substance—and to reserve that explicitness for exceptional cases only. I am fully conscious of the nature and effects of blessing and of its eternal substance, the knowledge of which has been entrusted to me. As a result, any description of the act of blessing could never simply be empty words to me. Thus, when you find words of blessing at the end of my letters, you can be certain that in each instance the act of blessing took place from within the eternal Spirit in which I dwell and is intended specifically for you as the rightful recipient of the letter. Each time you read this blessing anew, actively absorbing my words into your innermost being, its power will flow to you once again, even if decades have elapsed between readings.

Bear in mind that I am not blessing you because I was inspired to do so in response to something particular about you but, rather, because of your connection with my words—as one who has the ability to absorb these words. In my letters to you it has been my intention to also address such words to whoever may read them and is ready to absorb them within. Thus, such blessings will be felt by and will benefit anyone with whom you may share my letters, provided that they have developed to the point where they are able to receive true blessings.

I am presenting here facts for you to ponder, so that you may be as informed as possible about the nature of true blessing.

Real blessing is, as I have just mentioned, a spiritual energy that has *substance*. The power of that spiritual energy is modulated so that its intensity corresponds to the inner capacity of the person being blessed to receive it.

The power of blessing is not dependent upon a prayer or a wish, some special gesture by the person who is blessing, or on a phrase either spoken or thought. Rather, it is spiritual substance directed by the will of a spiritual entity who dwells in a physical body here on earth. This union of the spiritual being with a mortal body is necessary if a blessing is to have an effect not only on the spiritual but also on the physical being of the individual for whom the blessing is intended.

To my spiritual "eye" the blessing I bestow looks like a radiant white flame that I can only compare to the glow of radium when viewed under a microscope in a darkened room. The luminosity of this spiritual flame is incomparably more intense than that emitted by radium—so strong that, due to the reflex of protecting the body's eyes from overly strong light, I often close my physical eyes when I "see" it. This even though I am seeing with my "spiritual eye" that is, of course, accustomed to all intensities of spiritual light.

The act of blessing takes place through use of the *will* of those who have the ability to bless. This occurs as follows: The spiritual substance from which a blessing is to be formed is first seen by the bestower as an irregular, unformed radiant flame. By an act of will, this unformed flame is transformed into the spiritual form needed for the intended blessing. The blessing may be bestowed close by or sent beyond continents and oceans, in accordance with the will of the individual imparting the blessing. The blessing may also take effect multiple times, depending on how the blessing is willed.

In your letters you often emphasized that when you received my blessings you could feel them in a palpable, physical way. It was clear to you that these feelings were real and that you were not imagining things. I did not speak to these reports from you at the time because I knew you were not yet inwardly ready for the detailed discussion that would need to follow. I can now confirm that your perceptions have not deceived you. Through my blessing you have indeed received something "tangible": an energy that is purely spiritual yet has substance and is felt through the physical body. That spiritual energy is palpable, empowering, and enriching for you physically. I want to also point out that it is possible for you as recipient to reject a blessing, either consciously or unconsciously, through your inner bearing. The blessing then returns to the one who sent it, as if it had ricocheted off a granite wall.

As a being within the realm of Spirit, the radiant substance that holds the energy of blessings is as tangible and moldable to me as the sand used for casting in a foundry. Ever since the time I have been able to bestow blessings, I have consistently perceived their effect on the person blessed the moment the blessing was accepted. This knowledge comes to me as a tangible, spiritual energy that is experienced through my spiritual body.

As you can see, we are dealing here with something different from that which is commonly referred to as "blessing," such as when members of the clergy perform a ceremony consisting of certain formulaic benedictions and accompanying gestures, based on their supposed authority to bless. This sort of blessing will only be of value if the individuals performing the blessing are able to summon their fervent thoughts and channel them, through the power of will, to support the one being blessed. Any person is, of course, capable of doing this to a certain degree: The blessing parents bestow upon their child is the best example of this.

A real blessing originates in the realm of living, spiritual Light and the self of one who would bestow it must *be* in this same eternal Light and be gifted with the ability to make use of the substance that can be used for blessing. Such a person may never bestow a blessing upon himself; however, he will not suffer any deprivation because his being is suffused at all times by the blessings of others who are able to bless.

Now that you have been awakened to a certain degree as to what happens here, I solemnly bestow on you the blessing that is mine to bestow.

LETTER TWENTY-NINE

THE TIMELESS NATURE OF ETERNITY

IN YOUR LAST MOST WELCOME LETTERS I saw clear signs of a gradually growing and unmistakable, greater openness in your receptivity to matters of the Spirit, even at times when you had to struggle with the limitations of your earthly nature, or thought you still could not trust your perceptions. Your most recent account confirmed for me that you have progressed beyond what I could have dared to expect so soon. I can say with certainty that your spiritual eye has opened and that you have now begun to consciously experience your eternal self. It also comes as no surprise to learn that, although your soul is filled with joy, you feel unable to express your spiritual experience in words, such that everything you write to me feels to you like nothing more than an "inadequate stammer." Everyone who has had the same spiritual opening as you has come up against the same limitation and, for the most part, one must simply accept that the eternal cannot be expressed in words.

When we are trying to describe things in the earthly realm, the only way we can make ourselves intelligible to others is by *comparing* that which we want to describe to other things, and by using the established terminology of a given language. But when we are trying to describe an experience of the Eternal, fitting comparisons and terminology do not exist. And yet we feel the desire to express this experience in words—even if only for ourselves, even if only in our thoughts. Because adequate language does not exist, we resort to words that are meant for earthly matters, and force them to serve the purpose. And these words can only serve that purpose if we ignore their inadequacy and overlook the fact that there are no fitting comparisons in the earthly realm of existence.

The experience of Eternity is a ceaseless delving-into-the-depths of the eternal moment. In this eternal moment there is no "one event following the other" or "before and after" but, rather, a state of continuous spiritual-spatial interpenetration. Eternity is not an infinite number of events that follow each other but, rather, a *timelessness* that has no beginning or end and has always been so.

Those who are unable to experience this unending Eternity—unlimited and continuous as a circle—at every second in themselves can never understand any explanation, because all explanations take place in the realm of earthly time and thus can only be understood in terms of time. Those who have never lived in the realm of Eternity imagine it as an infinitely long amount of *time*. Even those who are qualified to speak of the timeless realm are forced to describe it by using the term "eternity"—which carries with it earthly connotations of an endless amount of time. I myself have even been forced to refer to immeasurably long periods of time—eons—as "eternities"—as if one could subdivide the infinite, unbreakable space-time that is Eternity.

For those who have not yet experienced the eternal realm within themselves, it is difficult to give up the mistaken notion that Eternity is the infinite ongoingness of *time*—and that this notion is the essence of what is meant by "the fullness of time."

As you now see, the Eternal eludes every attempt to understand its nature by comparing it to things in this realm of time. Eternity is different in its *essence* and is accessible only to the mode of perceiving that is unique to the eternal realm—and to which my books have led you without your noticing that this process was happening. But how many sketches from different points of view were necessary to gradually awaken a feeling in you for the timeless, spiritual space within you!

In my texts on spiritual matters I use a method that reminds me of certain drawings by Rembrandt, where the finished portrayal is based on countless marks on the page that gradually form the intended image. I explain Eternity by using many words on the page and it is impossible for me to do so in any other way if I am to bring about a dawning in the minds of my readers of what I wish to convey to them. And so it is for anyone who experiences eternal Reality.

Those who *know* Eternity need only the slightest allusion to a particular aspect to understand each other and know what is meant. You, however, have sketched out far more than just allusions and I must warn you not to try to portray your experience too clearly out of fear that I might miss something in your description.

May you remain in the Light and be blessed always.

LETTER THIRTY

SURRENDER AND INNER STILLNESS

YOU SAY—JOYFULLY—THAT YOU OWE your ability to experience the Spirit within yourself to the fulfillment of my "demands." I do not make demands: I offer. All can *choose* whatever speaks to them from that which I have brought. I merely point out what is required of seekers so that they may experience the radiant Spirit—prerequisites for spiritual unfolding that flow from the structure of life within the eternal Spirit itself.

You can only become God's cradle—your Living God can only be born within you—when you have learned to let go of all self-importance. This requirement is core and is by no means an arbitrary "demand." Any hope you harbor that you may still be allowed to keep some aspect of your consciousness for yourself bars the gate to your soul. God does not rent space; God will only enter as an *owner*. Thus you may not reserve even the smallest aspect of your consciousness as belonging to you. You must turn over everything you thought you might be able to keep to yourself and surrender it to your Living God. You must even surrender your consciousness to God if you are to become conscious of God.

Nothing is being demanded here; I am merely pointing out what is necessary to progress in the internal world so that you will not hope for impossible things, only to be disappointed later. In the external world you respect that there are conditions that must be fulfilled in order to accomplish a particular task; you know what is required as a result of your own and others' experience. As regards the eternal realm, however, you cannot gain this knowledge until *after* you have attained what you set out to attain. This is why you have to be shown what is required by someone whose consciousness reaches into the Eternal itself. Only in this way can you hope to experience what you strive for—and I am satisfied that you are well on the way now.

It was gratifying to read that you now feel with certainty that you are able to experience the

Eternal within yourself. As a result, you tell me that you have now realized that under no circumstances can one perceive with the physical senses the soul of someone who has died. You recognize that any manifestations of the life of those no longer in a physical body lie beyond what can be perceived by the physical senses. You should also recognize that these first experiences you are having of your newly awakening consciousness of the Eternal are also far removed from anything that can be experienced through the soul you have in common with other animals and through your physical senses.

For this very reason I must repeat the gentle warning at the end of my last letter and ask you, insofar as possible, to suppress your urge to compare your spiritual experiences to earthly experiences, because you think such comparisons will aid in my understanding. I will know what you mean even if you describe what you wish to impart in the barest outline.

Experiences in the realm of Eternity cannot be translated into language that is intended to describe experiences in the realm of time—not even if such language were expanded by the creation of thousands upon thousands of new words and terminology. The languages of this earth have developed in the realm of time in order to describe existence in the realm of time and cannot be bent to describe things that come to consciousness in a manner that shares no common ground with our physical realm. A repeated, stubborn attempt on your part to make the impossible possible might lead to a paralysis of your spiritual organs of perception—even before they have developed to the point where they could alert you to the danger your striving would bring to you. Your desire to express in language that which you are experiencing in your awakened consciousness is completely understandable; nevertheless, the end result could be destructive. Needless to say, I want to see you protected from this danger.

When you engage in inner conversations with yourself, do not imagine that you are speaking with God. God will only "speak" in you when you are able to remain completely still within. God will only "hear" you in your *stillness*. And never will God speak in words of a human language.

May you tread the path so recently opened to you with joy and steadfastness but also with care. May you receive every blessing that you need as you walk upon it.

God can only give to us
what we offer to be taken.
The magnitude of what God gives us
is determined by what we joyfully
surrender
valuing God's gifts
more than all possessions.

CONCLUSION

I strictly deny myself
the right to render judgment over things
that on this earth are not for me to judge.
I know for certain
that those of weight
as well as those of little weight
shall not escape the valuation
of their worth.

Everyone must one day without fail
reveal themselves before all
and stand on a scale that knows no error:
A day of judgment
determined by what one has become.

It would certainly have been possible for me to add many more letters to this book and I do not preclude the possibility that I might someday produce a second volume. But for now, the letters in this collection will suffice.

If this book awakens a desire in those readers for whom it is intended to read more such letters so as to further their development, then I have fulfilled the task I set for myself better than if I had written something more comprehensive. Indeed, more writings might have given readers too many details and hindered their ability to gain an overview of the whole. The reaction to my short pamphlet, "In My Own Behalf" has amply proven to me that clarity is not dependent on how many words an author uses but, rather, the ability to convey the essence of the subject at hand so that readers can take it in at a glance.

In this collection of letters I deliberately made no mention of the three syllables "Bô Yin Râ," which represent my eternal being in the medium of language. Many people who come across my books mistakenly believe these syllables to be a pseudonym and this name continues to be the object of endless misinterpretation. My reasoning for this omission is as follows: The organizing principle I followed in selecting and editing the letters for this book is the path of inner, spiritual development as it unfolds for those who embark upon it. This path is well known to me from the many individual cases that have come to my attention, along with the various detours it can take and the variations it may have. The individuals whose letters I used in compiling this book had already freed themselves from conventional, distorted ideas as to what these three syllables might signify, even before writing their first words to me. Thus, the correspondence that I have occasionally received concerning my name and the letters that "carry" its essence had no relevance for this book.

Yet, it would be irresponsible of me if at the end of this book I did not take up this topic—but there is no reason to do so in letter form.

Time and again the three syllables representing my eternal being are mistakenly thought to be in a foreign language because of their unusual spelling and pronunciation. Some believe my name to be of Indian origin but, in fact, these three syllables in no way correspond to any combination of letters or syllables used to create a name in India. The same is true for the various languages used to create names in China. I must ask Indologists and Orientalists to forgive me for mentioning something so obvious but, unfortunately, I am obliged to do so.

Had I wanted to create a pseudonym for myself it would have been bizarre for me to think of creating it from linguistic regions that have no connection whatsoever with me. It is public knowledge that I am of Frankish Mainz lineage, the descendant of peasant winemakers, foresters, and rural craftsmen. My outer life too, none of which has been hidden from view, has had nothing to do with foreign lands. Only an adventurous eccentric, estranged from his native European friends and family after having spent years abroad in Asian countries, could perhaps come up with the romantic idea of hiding behind a foreign pseudonym.

Such a person would have to be out of touch with the real world to think that this masquerade would be taken seriously by intelligent, modern Europeans. Everything I have ever written is intended solely for readers to whom a European hiding behind an Asian pseudonym would at best be tolerable in places of amusement—among circus performers or those who perform feats of daring. This is how I would react and I assume that others would feel the same way.

Moreover, I have made no secret of what these three syllables signify. I have never published a single line under this name that is equivalent to my eternal being, or even used just its initial letters, without informing many of those close to me about the spiritual circumstances that forbade me to credit to my family name writings that did not originate from that source. Additionally, long before I had published any books, I had gained enough insight into editorial and publishing practices to realize that, even if I thought a pseudonym were necessary, using one derived from Asian languages would be inappropriate. In any case, there was no reason whatsoever that would have motivated me to use a pseudonym.

Intelligent people everywhere will refuse to be taken in by some silly disguise and only an ignorant fool would think that taking a foreign name might intrigue readers and so advance his or her cause.

ꕥ

In a pamphlet published some time ago* I explained that the three syllables Bô Yin Râ are

* "Why I Use My Name" was a pamphlet first published in German in 1927 by the Kober'sche Verlagsbuchhandlung in Berne, Switzerland. It was first published in English in 1977 under the title "Concerning My Name" by The Kober Press,

not three words containing some secret meaning—even though they also correspond to linguistic roots in ancient languages. Rather, these seven letters constitute the name that is equivalent to my primordial, spiritual being because their phonetic qualities and the letters, when viewed as symbols, correspond to my eternal spiritual nature. It is as if each letter represents a specific musical note, which together correspond to a particular musical chord.

The "Y" in "Yin" is to be pronounced as "Ü,"* which is related to the Old High German "Win." The "Y" cannot be replaced by a "J."** The circumflexes above the "o" in Bô and the "a" in Râ are instructions to lengthen the vowel sound.

Berkeley, California, USA as part of a collection of Bô Yin Râ's essays entitled *Bô Yin Râ: An Introduction to His Works*. An edited version of "Concerning My Name" is available at The Kober Press website at http://kober.com under the heading "About Bô Yin Râ."

* Represented in the International Phonetic Alphabet by the phonetic symbol [y:].

** In German, the letter J is pronounced like the letter Y is pronounced in English.

In this same pamphlet I also explained how the spiritual instruction I had been receiving introduced me to the concept of a *true name*, which is different from the understanding of names that is common here on earth. I mentioned how, through the schooling of my soul, I had entered on the singular path that leads from one name to another, whereby certain letters of this name act like spiritual "antennae" through which spiritual help continually flows to the one being led in this direction.

For a long time I walked the path of names prepared for me and came to know, from my own experience, the power of a spiritual name to awaken inner energy. During my education, guided by the Spirit, I had borne a succession of such "names." I had to overcome each one in turn by overcoming *myself*, so as to at last be spiritually worthy of my true eternal name while still in my mortal, physical body. Of course, the pace of my inner development and the rhythm of its natural unfolding was determined by my obligation to first respond to the demands of everyday life.

❧

Within my eternal being, I have always been conscious of the reality that is expressed by the three syllables, Bô Yin Râ—but it took time for my earthly consciousness to become aware of it. However, even after I had already for some years been conscious in my earthly self of the spiritual substance of my eternal name, it seemed to me impossible to find a way to represent it in equivalent sounds and letters. But then, on a blessed night by the shore of the Hellenic sea, my spiritual mentor, who was united with my spirit and was gathered there among others who were also in union with my spirit, opened my eyes and ears to how this equivalency was possible—yes, even *necessary*—to accomplish. From that time forward I knew how to express in sound and symbols that which is my name in the radiant, timeless Spirit: an energy whose form is determined by the Father and which is eternally being generated in the realm of Spirit, through an unique impulse emanating from the Father's will.

This is the *real* secret behind the supposed Indian name which people mistakenly assume is a pseudonym of foreign origin.

Nothing exists in isolation in eternal Being, therefore too, nothing exists in isolation in earthly being. Thus, the name Bô Yin Râ, which is the earthly formulation that represents what I *am* in my eternal name, is also connected to other earthly things, with varying degrees of closeness. This is why some interpretations of these three syllables, when based on linguistic considerations—the sound and tonal qualities when spoken or some symbolism associated with the letters—contain more truth than those of any self-appointed "interpreters."

The idea that I would encourage more analyses of my name by suggesting possible associations that could be made with it—as has been often enough demanded of me—offends my sense of good taste. I hope that people can come to understand this. Those reading my books would not find it any easier to tread the path even if they knew exactly which ancient religious cultures had been spiritual homes to me at the time I was preparing for my earthly task. Nor would it be of the slightest use to seekers if they had discovered all the secret meanings—to which I myself am completely indifferent—of the letters contained in the three syllables, including the numeric values traditionally applied to these letters in various Asian and other ancient languages. One should not expect explanations from me about things which are of no importance to me in my own life, especially considering the little time I have available here on earth to perform the tasks given to me.

Those who cannot refrain from indiscriminately pursuing whatever byways they may come across while on their path to the Light will hardly, during their lifetime, reach the goal that may only be attained by resolutely staying on the path. Even the most high-minded quest for knowledge is nothing but seduction if it lures seekers off their path. I can hardly encourage pursuits that I know will impede seekers' progress. Alas, more important tasks demand my attention than the satisfaction of idle curiosity.

And so today, I end this book with the same intention as I wrote it. I bless those spiritually chosen by me to receive this book, from the realm of eternal Light and in my eternal name.

Bô Yin Râ

For a deeper understanding
of the core of Bô Yin Râ's teachings
you may want to read:

The Book on the Living God,
The Book on Life Beyond and
The Book on Human Nature

These three books should be
read together.

A description of all three books follows.

The Book on the Living God

The Book on the Living God describes the inner path that leads to birth of the Living God within—what we must do and what to avoid on the long journey towards awakening the consciousness of our timeless self.

Ordinary consciousness, Bô Yin Râ tells us, is actually like sleep; there is a greater consciousness that is alive in us, informing every cell, and our task is to unite it with our self-awareness.

We must also set aside the ideas we have been taught about an anthropomorphic God. God is not meant to be an external object of worship but, rather, an experience to be awakened within us. We are cautioned to avoid the pitfalls that might divert us: following false teachers or believing that certain foods or exercises, or ecstatic experiences, have spiritual merit. Everyday life, when lived with attention to the ultimate goal, will lead us towards a gradual awakening of our timeless self.

Contents: *Word of Guidance. "The Tabernacle of God is with Men." The White Lodge. Meta-Physical Experiences. The Inner Journey. The En-Sof. On Seeking God. On Leading an Active Life. On "Holy Men" and "Sinners." The Hidden Side of Nature. The Secret Temple. Karma. War and Peace. The Unity among Religions. The Will to Find Eternal Light. The Human Being's Higher Faculties of Knowing. On Death. On the Spirit's Radiant Substance. The Path toward Perfection. On Everlasting Life. The Spirit's Light Dwells in the East. Faith, Talismans, and Images of God. The Inner Force in Words. A Call from Himavat. Giving Thanks. Epilogue.*

The Book on Life Beyond

The Book on Life Beyond is a guide to help readers understand what they can expect to find in the life beyond death, and how to best prepare for it.

Bô Yin Râ explains that life beyond is actually another dimension of the same life we know here on earth—just as real and solid, but perceived through spiritual, rather than our limited, physical senses. He emphasizes the direct connection between our actions here on earth and their effects on life beyond. We bring with us into life beyond the same state of inner being with which we departed, and are able to experience its wonders exactly to the degree to which we have developed our spiritual self. For example, those who have failed to show compassion for others and have lived selfishly will find that life beyond lacks the warmth and light that other, more developed souls can perceive.

Bô Yin Râ counsels us to mentally practice the "art of dying" as a meditative practice to prepare for the transition from physical to spiritual existence. The goal is to constantly orient one's thinking, emotions and desires toward transformation of the self, in order to be able to receive the spiritual help that will be available to us after death.

Contents: *Introduction. The Art of Dying. The Temple of Eternity and the World of Spirit. The Only Absolute Reality. What Should One Do?*

The Book on Human Nature

The Book on Human Nature presents basic concepts about human nature with the goal of inspiring readers to awaken the timeless, spiritual spark within. We become fully human only when the spiritual potential within us gradually awakens and infuses our material, purely animal selves. It is a path that every human being may and should pursue.

A central understanding is that all life results from the joining of opposites, in particular, the polarity of male and female energies. Bô Yin Râ emphasizes that the true spiritual human being is male and female united in one entity; when we seek our spiritual self, we must call forth the male and female in ourselves and in all things. He discusses the biblical fall from grace as a descent from the spiritual plane, in which male and female were united, onto a material plane, in which male and female are split apart.

Bô Yin Râ warns men that holding onto the illusion of male superiority means forfeiting their spiritual life. While the spiritual paths that are natural for men and women are different in tone—open and receptive for women, active and grasping for men—they are equal and complementary. He tells us that *true* marriage is preparation for the life beyond: by coordinating the desires, wills and attitudes of two beings we once again bring about, in some measure, the original state in which male and female energies are united.

Contents: *Introduction. The Mystery Enshrouding Male and Female. The Path of the Female. The Path of the Male. Marriage. Children. The Human Being of the Age to Come. Epilogue. A Final Word.*

THE
KOBER
PRESS

www.ingramcontent.com/pod-product-compliance
Lightning Source LLC
LaVergne TN
LVHW091029080826
845145LV00002B/419